Praise for *Reveal*

"*Reveal* is one of the most uplifting, honest, exhilarating books I have ever read. I devoured every page of this beautifully written life-changing work. It speaks to the Divine embodied soul of every woman and leaves you as refreshed as a spring rain in the desert."

— **Christiane Northrup, M.D.**, OB/GYN physician and *New York Times* best-selling author of *Women's Bodies, Women's Wisdom* and *The Wisdom of Menopause*

"The Divine Feminine has found a beautiful voice in Meggan Watterson's new book, *Reveal: A Sacred Manual for Getting Spiritually Naked*. Written with a vulnerable heart and a fierce commitment to truth, Meggan's spiritual journey will inspire you to find and follow your own true soul-voice. I loved every single page!"

— **Cheryl Richardson**, author of *The Art of Extreme Self-Care*

"*Reveal* is a healing, a retelling, a remembering. The words fly like ignited prayer from the heart of Meggan Watterson. This book is a passionate calling to mend the desecrating separation between body and soul and make the world whole."

— **Eve Ensler**, founder of V-Day and *New York Times* best-selling author of *The Vagina Monologues* and *I Am an Emotional Creature*

"Meggan Watterson is a poet and a scholar and a real-life 21st century seeker. She's your best girlfriend . . . and a trusted spiritual guide suggesting shortcuts toward wisdom and happiness. This is a lovely book."

— **Elizabeth Lesser**, co-founder of the Omega Institute and author of *Broken Open: How Difficult Times Can Help Us Grow*

"The world is hungry for the awakening consciousness of the feminine spirit. Meggan's journey is riveting, magnificently told, and will help you to unlock your own."

— **Regena Thomashauer**, author of *Mama Gena's School of Womanly Arts*

"Meggan Watterson brings alive the concept of spirituality as something that is not separate from us, or something we have to go out and pursue or attain. I just love the way she weaves everything, from her sexuality, her body, her emotions—in fact, her life—into a seamless tapestry that teaches us the spiritual importance of being who we are, and that our life is our prayer to the universe. This is a book after my own heart!"

— **Anita Moorjani**, best-selling author of *Dying to Be Me*

"*Reveal* cracked me open, reawakened my spirit, and reminded me that I'm not alone on my spiritual journey. Meggan Watterson addresses so much of what we're afraid to say. This book opened my heart and fed my soul. *Reveal* is a blessing to the world."

— **Gabrielle Bernstein**, *New York Times* best-selling author of *May Cause Miracles*

"Watterson's voice is so powerful that when you open this book you will feel like she is sitting next to you, staring into your eyes over a cup of tea, and talking directly to you about all that matters in life. Even skeptics can't help but respond to such a brilliant, clear vision about waking up the voice you are meant to have. This spiritual memoir will reach straight into your soul and stay there."

— **Donna Freitas, Ph.D.**, author of *The End of Sex and Sex and the Soul: Juggling Sexuality, Spirituality, Romance, and Religion on America's College Campuses*

"Meggan Watterson reveals for us all the deep journey of self-love through the arms of the feminine. *Reveal* takes you on a soulful and sacred journey that will make you laugh, cry, and awaken the inner divine rebel living and breathing inside of you."

— **Christine Arylo**, self-love author and founder of Madly in Love with ME

"Meggan Watterson writes of the body, 'it is your chance to be here.' The same could be said of this book—it is a chance, a wish, a vision of a world where women's bodies and their spirits are united, where their pasts don't lock them in shame, where their futures are wide open and self-created. Meggan's fiercely original, unapologetically intense writing sucks you in from page one and doesn't let you go until you spin out from the end, changed."

— **Courtney E. Martin**, author of *Perfect Girls, Starving Daughters: How the Quest for Perfection Is Harming Young Women*

"Meggan Watterson writes from the white-hot place where two passionate inquiries intersect. She is a seeker, in the fullest sense, and her feminism runs just as deep. *Reveal* is a fireball of a book . . . Meggan is so adept at limning out a story that you come away feeling as if you'd read an engaging novella even as you were absorbing her remarkable seven-point program for claiming and reclaiming just about everything that matters!"

— **Carol Lee Flinders, Ph.D.**, author of *At the Root of This Longing: Reconciling a Spiritual Hunger and a Feminist Thirst* and *Enduring Lives: Portraits of Women and Faith in Action*

"Intimate, vulnerable, and courageous, Meggan Watterson's *Reveal: A Sacred Manual for Getting Spiritually Naked,* is a gift to liberate your spirit and set you free!"

— **China Galland**, *author of Longing for Darkness: Tara and the Black Madonna, The Bond Between Women,* and *Love Cemetery*

"This book is an invitation back to who you really are. Read it and be reminded. *Reveal* is a call to return to the essence of you, beautifully interwoven with stories that will make your soul sizzle in recognition."

— **Kate Northrup**, author of *Money: A Love Story*

"*Reveal* reminds us that we are sacred, that we must worship at our own inner altar, and that everyone has access to a mystical experience of life. Finally, spirituality from the embodied feminine perspective—this book is a touchstone for the next generation of women and their spiritual lives."

— **Alisa Vitti**, founder of FLOliving.com and author of *WomanCode*

Hay House Titles of Related Interest

YOU CAN HEAL YOUR LIFE, the movie,
starring Louise L. Hay & Friends
(available as a 1-DVD program and an expanded 2-DVD set)
Watch the trailer at: **www.LouiseHayMovie.com**

THE SHIFT, the movie,
starring Dr Wayne W. Dyer
(available as a 1-DVD program and an expanded 2-DVD set)
Watch the trailer at: **www.DyerMovie.com**

ARCHETYPES: Who Are You?, by Caroline Myss

*THE ART OF EXTREME SELF-CARE: Transform Your Life One
Month at a Time*, by Cheryl Richardson

MEDIDATING: Meditations for Fearless Romance,
by Gabrielle Bernstein

*THE TAPPING SOLUTION: A Revolutionary System for Stress-Free
Living*, by Nick Ortner

*WOMANCODE: Perfect Your Cycle, Amplify Your Fertility,
Supercharge Your Sex Drive and Become a Power Source*,
by Alisa Vitti

All of the above are available at your local bookstore,
or may be ordered by contacting Hay House (see next page).

REVEAL

REVEAL

A SACRED MANUAL FOR
GETTING SPIRITUALLY NAKED

Meggan Watterson

HAY HOUSE

Australia • Canada • Hong Kong • India
South Africa • United Kingdom • United States

First published and distributed in the United Kingdom by:
Hay House UK Ltd, Astley House, 33 Notting Hill Gate, London W11 3JQ
Tel: +44 (0)20 3675 2450; Fax: +44 (0)20 3675 2451
www.hayhouse.co.uk

Published and distributed in the United States of America by:
Hay House, Inc., PO Box 5100, Carlsbad, CA 92018-5100. Tel.: (1) 760 431 7695 or
(800) 654 5126; Fax: (1) 760 431 6948 or (800) 650 5115.
www.hayhouse.com

Published and distributed in Australia by:
Hay House Australia Ltd, 18/36 Ralph St, Alexandria NSW 2015. Tel.: (61) 2 9669
4299; Fax: (61) 2 9669 4144. www.hayhouse.com.au

Published and distributed in the Republic of South Africa by:
Hay House SA (Pty), Ltd, PO Box 990, Witkoppen 2068. Tel./Fax: (27) 11 467 8904.
www.hayhouse.co.za

Published and distributed in India by:
Hay House Publishers India, Muskaan Complex, Plot No.3, B-2, Vasant Kunj, New
Delhi – 110 070. Tel.: (91) 11 4176 1620; Fax: (91) 11 4176 1630.
www.hayhouse.co.in

Distributed in Canada by:
Raincoast, 9050 Shaughnessy St, Vancouver, BC V6P 6E5. Tel.: (1) 604 323 7100;
Fax: (1) 604 323 2600

Cover design: Johanna Goldfield, LLC • *Interior design:* Riann Bender

Reprinted by permission of the publisher and the Trustees of Amherst College
from *The Poems of Emily Dickinson: Variorum Edition,* Ralph W. Franklin, ed., Cambridge, Mass: The Belknap Press of Harvard University Press, Copyright © 1998 by
the President and Fellows of Harvard College. Copyright © 1951, 1955, 1979, 1983
by the President and Fellows of Harvard College.

Reprinted by permission of the translator. "We Three" by Jalal al-Din Rumi, *The
Essential Rumi,* trans. Coleman Barks with John Moyne, San Francisco: HarperSan-
Francisco ©1995 by Coleman Barks.

The Collected Poems of Muriel Rukeyser © 2005 by Muriel Rukeyser. Used by Permission. All rights reserved.

A catalogue record for this book is available from the British Library.

ISBN 978-1-84850-893-4

Printed and bound in Great Britain by TJ International Ltd.

*This book is dedicated to every woman
who desires to hear and follow
the soul-voice inside her.*

Contents

Invocation

i am the sex of human that has consumed the fruit,
the snake's offering.

and no, i am not guilty. and yes, i am naked.
and no, i am not ashamed.

and yes, i am that silhouette there in the distance,
the one always found dancing.

i am a scarlet letter, i am burned at the stake. my name is sita, i am a bride.
my name is thecla, i will never be married.

i am shaped like a triangle, i am as curved as the number three.
i am s-like and undulating. i am fire, and i taste of an ancient sea.

i am that feeling you had when you tried to forget me.

i am that moment when you eclipsed yourself, and suddenly
i am here—a shrine within you left too long unattended.

i am that impulse you had to light a candle there. yes,
i am this simple. yes, i come this easily.

for you, i will press myself flat like a book that has never been read.

i will hold myself there against your skin and watch as your eyes close
from the heat of me, so near to you.

i will let you handle me like a verse of sacred scripture,
i will entrust all of my pages for your beholding.

for you, i will open to the meatiest chapter of myself,
i will go straight to the pith, the real juice.

and i will say, "read here, beloved stranger, start sipping this nectar
for the soul journey of which you are now a pilgrim."

Introduction

Descent is not about finding light but about going into the darkness and befriending it. If we remain there long enough, it takes on its own luminosity. It will reveal everything to us.

—SUE MONK KIDD

"Do you know who you are?" the shaman asked.

A thick silence filled the short distance between us.

"Do you know who you are?" she repeated, her eyes locking mine so forcefully she might as well have put her hands on either side of my face. Responses were racing through me like the reels of a slot machine. But I remained silent as huge tears started to slide down my cheeks.

I knew who I was, but I had no idea how to express it. I didn't know how to mirror on the outside the truth of who I was within.

I had come to the shaman because I ardently believed she could flip a switch and change me. I believed that I would meet something or someone outside of myself—the right word, a wise thought, a sacred text, a spiritual master—that would touch my soul, and that would be it. Boom. I would be aligned with the truth of who I am. I would again be connected to that sense of love and freedom I knew without question as a little girl.

I was in my early 20s, and I knew what my life so far had cost me. I was afraid, not all the time but often enough that I allowed fear to dictate my choices. The most visible example was my fear of flying, which had morphed into a full-blown phobia. I couldn't be trusted when it came to planes. I jilted flights at the last minute like the Runaway Bride. I didn't want to believe that I was going to let fear decide where I could and couldn't go, so I would say yes to a trip and buy a ticket. I would even board the plane. But at the last minute, I would bolt for the door, leaving my family members or friends slack-jawed in the wake of my exit. By this point, I felt defeated. Confined. I had accepted that my life would have to remain *par terre*.

When a plane had taken off without me, and fear had released its grip, I would stand in the airport wondering what the *bleep* just happened. Fear, without fail, would turn out to be what wasn't actually true for me. Fear derailed me in other, more ordinary ways nearly every day. Moments when I wanted to say or do something but a doubt or a disbelief in myself would give fear the thumbs-up to come swooping in and stifle what I had wanted to share.

I had no idea how to feel at ease in my own skin, fully embodied and unafraid. And I wanted that freedom more than anything. Not just on flights and in difficult moments but all the time. I wanted to find a way to turn inward no matter what my external circumstances or how much fear I was experiencing, and know what is true for me, the actual rock of who I am. Not the smoke and shadow the ego emits, but a source more stable and constant.

There's a famous BBC interview in which the Swiss psychiatrist Carl Jung is asked if he believes in God. "Difficult to answer," he tells the interviewer. And then after the most perfect pregnant pause he says, "I *know*. I don't need to believe. I *know*." This is what I wanted. I wanted to *know* God, intimately. I wanted a personal experience of the Divine. I wanted to meet what is most sacred, not just one day a week or on holidays or on special occasions like weddings and deaths. I wanted the Divine to infuse every part of my life, every day, every breath.

Just as medicine—and later, psychology—were grounded in the male body and the male experience, the liturgy and spiritual practices of most of the world's religions were codified and created by men. I marched out of my Unitarian church at age ten after reading the Bible for the first time and realizing that women's voices weren't a part of the story. I have wondered since then what a spirituality would look like if it were created with women's experience and perspective in mind.

I wanted to be spiritual in a way that allowed me to be as at home in my soul as I am in my skin. Separating my sexuality from my spirituality didn't work for me, because it wasn't true to my experience. For me, it was only by winning back my body—by daring to really be present to all I was feeling in my body—that I finally began to connect to what is eternal in me. The body then wasn't an obstacle but, in a way, the goal.

I have spent the majority of my life gathering stories of the Divine Feminine. Each time before getting masters degrees in theology and divinity, I went on a pilgrimage to sacred sites of the Divine Feminine throughout Europe. The first was with a group and the second was on my own. So it went group pilgrimage, Master of Theological Studies, solo pilgrimage, Master of Divinity.

Through the stories of the Divine Feminine in Christianity's Mary Magdalene, Catholicism's Black Madonna, Hinduism's Kali Ma, and Buddhism's Green Tara, for example, I began to see that I wasn't as much of a spiritual misfit as I had thought. There was a red thread that became visible to me. It ran through many of the world religions, especially through their mystics, relaying that the way to find the Divine is to go within. And, that our potential to be transformed by going inward is exactly the same whether we are a man or a woman. The real barometer of our spiritual potential is not our sex, but the commitment of our desire to want to encounter the Divine.

In divinity school and seminary I came across early Christian writings that are not well known in the mainstream, such as *The Gospel of Mary Magdalene* and the *Pistis Sophia*. These are texts in which the Divine isn't out there, above or beyond us, but rather within us. And the central figures of these texts are women.

These were the voices that as a little girl I sensed were missing from the Bible. But what I really wanted to find was a text that helped me go within. I loved the metaphors of what happens by turning inward: the mystical union, the sacred marriage, the alchemical uniting of opposites. That all sounded so intriguing, so alluring, but I had no idea what any of it really meant or how to get there.

What I lacked most and longed to find was a sacred guide to the inner terrain. I needed help in navigating that unknown inner world, a person who could light my way through the darkness. I loved listening to sermons, homilies, and dharma talks, and attending satsangs, pujas, and midnight masses. I loved learning about saints, mystics, gurus, shamans, and holy people from around the world and in all traditions. But what I really craved was a sort of priestess to the churches and synagogues that travel within us wherever we go. I needed someone who could point me toward the holy temple that we can't see with our eyes but can only sense with our souls.

This, I found, is who I am.

To me being spiritual is less about learning something new and more about remembering what I have always known. Being spiritual is a process of stripping down to what is authentic for me, for my life. Getting spiritually naked is about having the courage to be radically open about the truth of who we are with no exceptions and no apologies, to reveal ourselves without judgment or shame.

Take Salome's seductive dance in the Bible as described in Matthew, starting around verse 14. Salome begins to shed the first of seven veils as she dances with hips and passion to win the favor of her uncle King Herod in order to then ask for John the Baptist's head. Such is the power of a woman revealing herself in public.

Like many good stories in the Good Book, the Dance of the Seven Veils has pre-Christian roots. It is thought to have originated with the great Babylonian goddess Ishtar. The story starts with Ishtar's seemingly innocuous wish to visit her sister, Ereshkigal, in the underworld. As Isthar descends, the gatekeeper will only let her through each of the seven gates if she will shed an article of clothing. Each discarded piece gets Ishtar nearer to her sister, and when she passes through the seventh gate, she is totally naked.

The seven veils that Salome slides off her skin and the seven gates Ishtar passes through can be seen as seven stages of a spiritual process. The more we reveal of ourselves, the closer we come to unveiling the soul, to reaching the Divine.

Seven is a favorite number among mystics, alchemists, and spiritual writers throughout history. There is the seven-headed red dragon in the Book of Revelation. There's St. Teresa's Interior Castle with "seven mansions" in which God meets her "from behind a shut door." There is the Trappist monk Thomas Merton, who equates the spiritual path to climbing a "seven storey mountain," and there is Deepak Chopra, with his "seven spiritual laws of success," just to name a few.

And then there is Marguerite Porete, a French mystic from the Middle Ages, who ascends through seven stages on her soul's journey to find union with Divine Love. She was encouraged by Church authorities to write down her experience, which she did, in her spiritual masterpiece, *The Mirror of Simple Souls*. Sharing her soul's story had dire consequences, however. After a lengthy trial that brought to the stand many of the foremost Church authorities (it's a given they were male), Marguerite and her *Mirror* were both deemed heretical and sentenced to death.

They burned her book first before burning Marguerite at the stake in Paris in 1310. My heart started to race when I read this. Not because she had been burned at the stake—a precursor to the witch hunts that would follow in the next century—but because of the fear her story invoked. To think that it was so threatening to church fathers for a woman to meet Divine Love inside her that they felt it necessary to destroy both her body and her book. Truth can never be silenced, however. Like the legend of the phoenix, Marguerite Porete's voice rises from the ashes to live on through *The Mirror of Simple Souls:* "But I was, says this Soul, and I am, and I will be always without lack, for Love has no beginning, no end, and no limit, and I am nothing except Love."[1]

Marguerite Porete wrote her spiritual memoir for the nuns of her abbey. She wrote down the seven-layered process of her spiritual transformation to meet with Divine Love within her because of her love for them. Through a women's spirituality group I have facilitated for over ten years, the REDLADIES, and through a women's spirituality conference I founded called REVEAL, I have met you—a whole different kind of holy woman. Smile.

Like Porete's seven-layered journey of spiritual transformation, the seven veils of *Reveal* are the seven stages of the spiritual process I went through, a process that stripped away what was no longer serving me, the false beliefs that covered up the truth of who I am.

If I could give you a visual of these seven stages, they would each be within the other like a Russian matryoshka doll, like concentric circles, or a seven-course unicursal labyrinth. And in the process I describe, the stages are not hierarchical; one is not more important than the other. They are not sequential; the soul does not reveal itself in linear fashion, although for the purposes of this book, I describe the stages in a certain order. Each veil moves back in time to the events and people in my life that helped to shift my beliefs at a particular stage of the process.

I refer to this book as "a sacred manual" because it contains what I have spent nearly two decades searching for: the sacred texts and spiritual voices of women. Discovering these stories, texts, and spiritual voices of the Divine Feminine helped me to reveal my own spiritual voice. I have found what I set out to know: a direct experience of the Divine. Whether I'm seated before a lighted candle, calm and serene, or I'm plowing my way through a crowded street in downtown New York City, I can feel and know what is Divine, what is true for me. And this is what I want most for you; to hear and feel the limitless love and wisdom of the truth inside you, to know and trust the voice of your own soul so much that you let it guide you from within.

What I want the spiritual process revealed in this book to give you is what it gave to me: a sense of **empowerment** that allows you to shed any feeling of being a victim and own everything that has happened to you; a feeling of **embodiment** that allows you to let go of every notion about the body except that it's sacred; an awareness of **true love** as a limitless source within you, not something or someone outside you; a feeling of **self-worth** that lets you accept that love is your birthright, not something you must prove yourself worthy of; the **audacity and authority** to know that you don't need to keep your power hidden, that we all have a direct connection to the Divine; a belief in service and **meaningful work** in the world that doesn't deplete you but rather demands that you receive as much as you give; an experience of the love and support of **spiritual community**

to remind you again and again that you're not alone—
that women do the work of saving each other's lives.

I want this book to be the spiritual mentor that I
couldn't find but desperately longed for when this process began for me. I want you to know that there is a
way through fear. You are not crazy for wanting so much
more out of life. You are not selfish or greedy either.

You have been initiated.

The First Veil

REVEAL Your Soul-Story

You own everything that happened to you.
Tell your stories.

—ANNE LAMOTT

THE INVISIBLE BRIDGE

I'm going to tell you a story. You've heard it before. It's really the only soul-story that has ever been told.

It starts with restlessness, a longing for more.

Or it starts with flashes of blinding light from an elusive pot of gold, streaks of an unreliable happiness dependent on something—a drug, a lover, a physical object—that reminds you of a light that's more lasting and then fades away.

Or it starts with a fire: a divorce or a death tears open the smallness of your life and reveals that something—a vastness—is impossibly near. And always has been. The bridge between you and that vastness is invisible yet you try everything to find it. You see this guru, you hear that imam. You travel to a shrine at the peak of some pass out–high mountain with a name you can't pronounce. You chant mantras. You have no sex. You have tantric sex. You sleep to interpret your dreams, and then you meditate with Buddhists to awaken.

You search the world to find the treasure you can sense is right here nearby, like your shadow. It is elusive and yet as ordinary and essential as the air you breathe. You go everywhere in search of this treasure, not realizing that what you are searching for is with you all the time. Finally, out of exhaustion, disillusionment, and sheer hopelessness, you stop. You end your search.

You come home.

You return to your just-okay life, to your so-so job, to your friends who sometimes love you and sometimes leave you too much alone. Then one day it dawns on you: there's still a place you haven't looked. You stand in the center of your shabby little studio apartment. You don't have everything you wanted for yourself. You have maybe very little of what you had imagined for yourself at age 13 but you're smiling anyway. For the first time in your life you see that there's absolutely no reason, no crisis, no something you lack that could keep you from letting that smile break open your face.

Your smile is not the vastness you were searching for, but it's a start. It's a glimmer of the pot of gold you were restless to find, the Promised Land, the "lost" treasure—that certain immutable something that no one and nothing can disturb or take from you no matter what comes your way. It's your own inner Shangri-La. It's your freedom.

In any given moment, in any situation life hands you, you can stand very still in the center of yourself and know what exists within you. You have the power to access it as easily and effortlessly as taking this next breath.

This is the story that so many of us keep living out—the inexorable search to find what we can never be without and have, in fact, never lost.

A psychic once told me that I would find true love in the most unexpected place. She was right.

I did. Within.

SEEING RED

I probably had a stomachache. Maybe I had eaten something too heavy for my digestive system the night before the Kali dream. I'm sure there's a rational explanation for why I can still remember the physical sensation, the actual weight of the Hindu goddess Kali standing on my body with one foot in my gut and one over my heart, as if striking a yogic warrior pose above me.

I had been studying Kali in one of my religion courses at Smith College. My mentor at the time had urged me not to choose Kali as the subject of my senior thesis. "Kali," she warned, "is a dangerous subject."

Kali is the Hindu goddess of Tantra, spiritual practices and rituals that aim to dissolve the dichotomy of sacred versus mundane so that every aspect of a Tantrika's life can be perceived as Divine. Kali is the consummate consort of the god Shiva. Together they destroy illusion to initiate spiritual transformation. Kali is known for her chaotic, wild dance, which only ends when she realizes she has danced right on top of Shiva's naked and erect man-body. At that point she sticks out her tongue as a gesture of having been calmed but not tamed.

This is the moment in Kali's infamous sacred story that I was experiencing in my dream. I was Shiva, and Kali was dancing on top of me, her red tongue reaching down to her chin. But what did it mean?

A lucid dream is one in which we're conscious that we're dreaming while still in the dream. At the time of the Kali dream, I was reading William James's *The Varieties of Religious Experience*. James writes about the conversion experience, the moment when a person is indelibly altered by an encounter with the Divine. The Kali dream converted me, though not to some form of Hinduism or Goddess worship.

Consider the iconography of Kali and Shiva. I know it's hard not to think that because Kali has breasts and because Shiva's erect that Kali is female and Shiva male. What they represent, and bear with me here, is the spiritual goal for us each to achieve. We are meant to look at them together, to consider them as a whole. And we are each meant to contain the union of them both. My Kali dream was an embodiment of this balance, so desperately needed not just individually but also collectively.

At some point, and if you're a historian or cultural anthropologist perhaps you know when, we assigned the masculine to men and the feminine to women. Each sex had to drop anchor with just that one attribute. And when it came to the Divine, to what was actually practiced and perceived as sacred, as a world culture, religions had deified just one sex, just one gender.

So my conversion experience was not to a particular religious tradition but rather to the vision of what was missing or out of balance in nearly all of them.

Since the Kali dream, red has become more than just a color to me. Now it is charged with far more meaning. It represents the sacredness of the body, birth, and sexuality. It represents the generosity of a broken-open heart that radiates unfaltering love like an uncapped fire hydrant. Red represents the kind of love that reaches the places where we are most broken and most vulnerable. Red is the color of Mary Magdalene's cape, the goddess Kali's tongue, and Dinah's tent or menstrual hut, in the Torah. With the Kali dream, red, for me, became a sacred reminder of the truth I had been converted to—that the Divine is also feminine.

Despite my mentor's warning about Kali, I was convinced the right goddess had found me. A goddess who was all woman—fully in her body, yet also Divine. A goddess who seemed to roar, "I am my own."

THE GODDESS IN EXILE

Let me show you a picture. The year is 1999. I'm 25 years old and about to enter divinity school. I am in the saw-toothed mountains of Catalonia, Spain, on a group pilgrimage to sacred sites of the Black Madonna and Mary Magdalene, led by China Galland, author of *Longing for Darkness: Tara and the Black Madonna*. It's a stifling hot Spanish May, considered "Mary's month" in the Catholic tradition.

The Black Madonna is an iconic depiction of the Virgin Mary with dark skin. There are an estimated 500 Black Madonnas throughout Europe, the majority dating back to the medieval period or earlier. This particular Black Madonna, in the Santa Maria de Montserrat Monastery, is most likely from the 12th century. Installed in an altar of gold, she is referred to as Rosa d'Abril, the Rose of Dawn.

After seeing the Black Madonna along with busloads of other pilgrims, China and I steal away from the rest of the group and climb to the hermitage high in the finger-like ridges of the mountain that reaches up behind the cathedral. China lets me approach the hermitage first. It is a weathered-looking place, and as I near it, I imagine being a monk there, with a small room in which to be alone with the Divine. The hermitage's heavy doors are shut with a chain and padlock, but each door panel has a tiny window. I pull myself up by the iron bars that cover one of the windows, so I can peek inside. This is when China takes the picture.

I'm craning my neck to get a look inside at what such solitude with the Divine would be like. There's a hint of desperation in my arms straining to hold me up before the view. I'm staring into the hermitage and thinking that at that moment, it contains all I need: a mattress, a blanket, some candles, and a small wooden chair. The roof of the hermitage is caving in, and thick beams of light are falling on the floor from above.

What I can't see as I'm pressed up against the window is what China's photo revealed to me when I finally saw it months after returning from the pilgrimage. There, next to my skinny little arms holding fast to the iron bars, are the letters G-O-D scratched into the hermitage door. God is on the same side of the locked door as I am.

Hold on to that visual for a moment.

As the legend goes, the Black Madonna of Montser-rat, a wooden statue of the Virgin Mary with Jesus as a child seated in her lap, was found in the strange, saw-toothed ridges at the top of the mountain. The Spaniards who found her knew that she was a powerful icon and wanted to bring her down the mountain to their cathedral, closer to what is now the city of Barcelona. But every time they tried to carry the Black Madonna down the mountain, the icon would increase in weight. The farther they descended, the heavier she became.

Finally, in a last attempt, they had the strongest men in Spain carry her down. They were almost at the bottom when the Madonna became as heavy as the mountain itself. The men had no choice but to carry her back up, and the higher they climbed, the lighter she became. They realized at last that the Black Madonna of Montserrat wanted to remain on the mountain. She wanted her cathedral built there in the sacred ridges that are said to have emerged from the earth at the moment Jesus was crucified.

At the time, I had a proclivity for what I refer to as being "kneed." Something would buckle my knees, explode my once normal-sized heart, and render me speechless and motionless for long periods of time, in a state of unfaltering love.

As I stood at the locked door to the hermitage, I wanted nothing more than to just be able to meet with the love that came in floods from somewhere within me. But I wasn't made to be a renunciate, to be sexless. As much as I wanted to be in that strange, unbounded love state, I wanted just as much to be entirely and fully in my body.

So even though I longed to find a quiet, dark space to be alone with the Divine, G-O-D scratched on the outside of the hermitage door told me it was time to come down from the mountain. It was time to come out of the wilderness, out of caves and recluses that set the spiritual apart from the physical, material world. It was time to make *all* of my life a spiritual practice, to be a mystic in the middle of traffic and a saint at the local supermarket.

And most important, it was time to consider sacred what had been "locked out" of organized religion—the body, especially the female body, and the Divine Feminine the female body represents. It was time to claim what had been exiled from holy terrain.

The definition of a pilgrim is one who embarks on a quest for something sacred. This is what I understood myself to be: a pilgrim on an inexorable quest to find a spiritual home.

As we descended in the tour bus from the hermitage high in the mountains, I felt heavy, like a spiritual misfit, a reluctant pilgrim who perpetually felt twice her age. Like the Black Madonna, I wanted to be carried back up the mountain. I didn't want to leave.

The irony of being kneed was this: the love blasted a crater wide enough to fit the whole universe inside my heart, yet oddly, at the same time it left me feeling epically alone, as though I would never belong and never find my own way of being in the world.

China often sang as we traveled from one pilgrimage site to the next. So as we wound our way down the mountain, she had us in pairs singing rounds of the children's song "Row, Row, Row Your Boat." Each time, I somehow ended up singing "Life is but a dream" on my own. (And I'm tone deaf with a great diaphragm. Not a fortunate combo.)

At one point I asked China what to do. Where should I go to worship, and with whom? Where does a pilgrim to the Divine Feminine find a mentor, a priestess, a she-pope?

China said with a smile, "You have to row a boat without oars."

As she said that, I saw myself rowing a small, red boat, my arms flapping about on either side of me. It made me think of the moment in *Indiana Jones and the Last Crusade* when Indie has to step into the chasm and trust that the bridge will rise up to meet his feet. He has to move forward out of faith and love, and only then does the invisible bridge appear to take him across the abyss to the waiting chalice.

I thought of how cryptic the spiritual journey seems at the start, how disbelief plagues us when we follow a tug that comes only from within. And how ultimately these stories are about being guided by something we can't see and needing to exercise that particular trust we have to cultivate in order to hear the unassuming voice of the truth inside us.

I didn't know how I would find a way. There was only the wild, broken-open love I felt while on my knees. There was only following that love blindly and trusting without proof that I should trust that at some point the oars would join the effort of my arms.

SAME-OLDS

I have always imagined that my desire to meet with true love, Divine Love, existed like a lighthouse within me, sending out a beacon in all directions to pull toward me what in the depths of my soul I wanted to meet most.

At first I believed that this true love I most wanted to meet was a tall, dark, and handsome hunk of a man.

A man who would see me and, in the instant our eyes met, would recognize me as the one he had been searching for, waiting for, finding his way toward all his life. The idea was so clear and so compelling that I was a lady-in-waiting to my real life. I was waiting for the arrival of this someone who would usher in a time when my outside matched who I really am on the inside. I was waiting for his arrival to *really* begin living.

Disempowering does not even begin to describe it.

I got my love-at-first-sight moment almost immediately after I began to pray for it. But it came in a way that I didn't recognize as "true love," a.k.a. my Tall, Dark, and Handsome. "He" was a she, and she looked just like me. Her eyes were impossibly similar to mine. It wasn't just that our eyes are very nearly the same color blue. It was less about their physical appearance and more about the way her soul seemed to look out through them that made me stare. Looking at her was like gazing into a crazy mystical and mysteriously sacred mirror.

I didn't feel as though I was meeting her for the first time. I felt as though I recognized her, but from where, I couldn't say. It was a knowing too deep to reach with conscious reasoning. We were meeting again, something in me whispered, and we had work to do, soul-work.

At the time, I saw myself as a victim without even being aware of it. And if someone suggested that I wasn't, I got really worked up, feeling that I was being blamed for the suffering in my life. I would plug my ears and put up my metaphysical dukes if I came across a person or spiritual teaching that suggested I create my own reality. Who the hell would choose abuse? Pain? Abandonment? A victim lives primarily in fear. And fear had me in a cage so small that my body couldn't fit inside it. I knew this had to change, that *I* had to change, but I didn't know how. Becoming conscious of my sense of victimization felt like trying to see the center of my own back.

Snow Flower and the Secret Fan, a novel by Lisa See, is set in 19th-century China when girls had their feet bound and spent their lives in seclusion, often with only a single window from which to catch a glimpse of the world they would never be able to enter. These women developed their own secret language, Nushu, the only gender-based language ever created. Some of the women were paired at a young age with another young woman, a "same-old," in an emotional relationship. These same-olds would send messages to each other in Nushu, written on fans or embroidered into handkerchiefs, surreptitiously sharing their stories.

I had met my same-old. And because of our relationship, I began to see the one window I had been looking out of, and I realized how trapped I had allowed myself to become.

One of the definitions of a miracle is simply to make wonderful. And according to *A Course in Miracles,* a guide to spiritual transformation, a miracle is simply "a shift in perspective." Loving my same-old was a practice of loving myself once removed. It was my first taste of self-love—self-love on training wheels. Meeting my same-old allowed me to feel for the first time in my life that I wasn't alone. Our souls spoke Nushu incessantly, silently conveying sentiments of love and encouragement. If I could condense a decade's worth of letters, e-mails, phone calls, and Skype between us, I would tell you that all my same-old ever said to me was "Begin."

My same-old and I were asked by a classmate in divinity school to pose as goddesses for a project. She was

Lakshmi, goddess of prosperity, and I was the goddess Kali. My dress was a red cloth wound tightly around my body and draped over one shoulder like a toga. I wore a thick silver belt with small bells dangling from it and there was a third blue eye painted between my eyebrows. When I went through what I call the Double Divorce, separating from my same-old and my Tall, Dark, and Handsome at the same time, I could have broken. Some part of me could have died for good. Instead, a miracle happened: I could see the center of my own back.

Now, when I look at the picture of my same-old and me on the day we were goddesses together, I can see how fierce I am. I can see what I didn't know how to claim at the time—that no matter how much I identified with being a victim, with being betrayed or abandoned, or how long or how often I moved from a place of fear, I was also this raw and brutal clarity. I was this immeasurable power. I was the author of my own story.

I was a deity dressed as a human, who could call forth all she desired.

SACRED SEX

When nearing traditional ideas of the sacred, there's an unspoken ultimatum: Leave your body, especially your female body, at the door. Take off your passion, your emotions, and especially your breasts and enter with only your calm, clean soul. Leave no traces of your human existence, of what formed your idea of the Divine to begin with.

I wore loose-fitting shirts that slid down my shoulder and tight designer jeans, and I always had on a bit of makeup—maybe some red lipstick one day and some mascara the next. This was holy work I was doing. In divinity school, a place that had for centuries been reserved only for men, I wasn't hiding my femininity or my sexuality. I wasn't wearing my sexuality on my sleeve as a commodity, or to be in vogue, or because of the pervasive imperative to be sexy that society has impressed upon my generation. I wore my sexuality with the audacious knowledge that the body is a holy temple.

The majority of the world religions have a negative message about the body, the female body in particular. Say the word "flesh" and the word "sin" appears in most of our minds, as if it were the flip side of it. My experience of being female contained the full spectrum from trauma to bliss. But I knew one thing with utmost certainty: that my body, my female body, brought me closer to the Divine, not further away from it. And though this was not the common view held in sacred scriptures the world over, I wore my sex with the knowing that it had everything to do with my own approach to the Divine.

I refuse to leave my body at the portico of the sacred. I refuse to separate my sexuality from my spirituality.

The goddess Isis, whose name means She of the Throne, was worshipped in ancient Egypt as the ideal wife and mother. She was the protector of everyone from aristocrats and rulers to slaves and prostitutes. Her sanctuaries lined the Nile delta in the millennia before the Common Era. She is most often depicted in hieroglyphs down on one knee with her arms outstretched and flanked by golden feathers.

Isis's story is morbid but captivating: her lover (and brother), Osiris, was murdered and then dismembered. Isis searched tirelessly for the lost pieces of his body, which had been scattered all over the earth. When she at last found all of them, she brought him back to life. The priests and priestesses who officiated at the sacred rites and rituals in Isis's temples were considered healers like her. To be initiated by the goddess Isis is to be initiated into magical powers to bring health, to restore life.

A theologian, I found, is much like an archeologist. Both develop expertise in digging. An archeologist sifts through sediment to find objects buried long ago, and a theologian sifts through words, trying in vain to find the first word, the real truth, and not some edited version of it.

I went to divinity school with the belief that there is a connection between our ideas of the Divine and the status of women, and that until there is a more balanced perception of the Divine as both male and female, masculine and feminine—or even better, beyond description—women and girls will continue to be mistreated by both themselves and others. I ardently believe that if men and women could speak with equal spiritual authority about the Divine, there would be far less gender-based violence in the world.

I became a theologian to find the missing stories of the Goddess that have been scattered all over this earth. I wanted to understand how exactly she was buried beneath this weight of the one God, the singular He. How had the Goddess been dismembered so completely? This is what liberated me from the epic, often debilitating anger I felt because women had been silenced for so long in all the major world religions.

My anger came from a belief that the days of the temple priestesses were forever erased and forgotten. As if there was a time of priests and priestesses, gods and goddesses, that could never come again. As if the time when the Divine was invested equally in all living things would remain in the past. When now here we are again, in a time that wants to remember that the female body is sacred.

The Goddess has always had a corner on resurrection.

THE BELOVED

In Hinduism, there's a spiritual path that's open to anyone. The sole requirement is that you feel intense, personal love for the Divine. This devotional worship is called *Bhakti*. In Bhakti, the Divine is experienced directly: it isn't distant and transcendent but intimate and immanent. This present, personal, cherished divinity is referred to as a Bhakti's *Ishta-deva,* or *Ishta-devata.* For a Bhakti, actions speak loudly, but sincere, genuine emotion creates a through line straight to the Divine.

Traditional Hinduism categorizes five different *bhavas,* or emotional expressions that characterize the devotional path of a Bhakti. There is *santa,* placid or gentle saintly love for the Divine; *dasya,* the attitude of a servant toward the master; *sakhya,* the attitude of a friend; *vatsalya,* the attitude of a mother toward her child; and *madhura,* the attitude of a woman toward her lover. The 19th-century mystic Ramakrishna practiced all five of these bhavas with the goddess Kali as his Ishta-deva, to experience the Divine directly.

The fifth bhava, the madhura bhava, that of a woman toward her lover, is what captivated me. And here's why—the word *beloved.* I was transfixed by it. Whether I came across it in the Bhakti poetry of the 15th-century mystic Kabir, in the mystical writings of the 16th-century saint Teresa of Avila, or in the writing of the 19th- and 20th-century poet Rainer Maria Rilke, it affected me physically. I read the word *beloved,* and my heartbeat suddenly became audible. My thoughts stopped. Emotion swept through me, pulsing with a heat and energy I couldn't explain or ignore. The word *beloved* altered my chemistry. It was as if honey were coursing through my veins.

And even more than the word *beloved,* addressing the Divine directly with the intimacy of a lover utterly undid me. "I am filled with you," writes the 13th-century Sufi mystic Rumi in a poem to the Divine. "Skin, blood, bone, brain, and soul." This love is so complete, Rumi confesses, that "there's no room for lack of trust, or trust."[1] There is only "this existence" when he and the beloved are one.

I had been journal writing since I was a little girl, ceaselessly recounting the significantly insignificant happenings of each day. But rather than recount every detail as if to some anonymous, distant self, as I had been, I began to write in my journal as if to the beloved. To *my* beloved. I switched from black ink to red and let each journal entry become a letter I was writing to the elusive and overpowering love I experienced while being kneed. I let that love become something intimate and personal. In other words, I was a Bhakti assuming a madhura bhava, with the beloved as my Ishta-deva.

When I started this practice of writing directly to the Divine, there were two things I didn't expect: one, that this seemingly innocuous and sometimes monotonous practice would have the force to transform my entire life, and two, that I would get a response.

Let me explain. As the practice of writing these love letters to the Divine continued—as I shared my most pressing desires and perplexing questions—I would find myself, at the end of some of my journal entries, writing a response to myself, as if in a trance. The voice that was addressing me directly was so fiery, so unburdened, so foreign to me that I felt compelled to write every day. At times the words would come in such a rush that it was hard for my hand to keep up. My heart throbbed as I wrote. I read each entry as if I were receiving a message, an answer, a clue. It felt like a voice that had been denied or held mute for centuries. Sometimes it felt like my voice, but mostly it felt like a voice that spoke through my red ink, conveying a spiritual fire that was older than writing itself.

The voice was filled with truth and paradox, and never failed to give me the answers I needed. It was like meeting an inner spiritual whippersnapper who knew my every weakness, my every fear, yet loved me fiercely still. How did I know when I was writing a response? The voice addressed me as the beloved, as "my beloved stranger."

It was through this journal-writing practice, through meeting this voice in my red ink, that just before graduation from divinity school, I became convinced that instead of returning to work as a counselor for pregnant teens, I needed to go on another pilgrimage to the Divine Feminine—to the sacred sites of the Black Madonna and Mary Magdalene that I had visited before I began divinity school. But this time, I needed to go on my own. I wanted to let this voice I was meeting in my journal guide me. I wanted to begin taking that voice seriously.

After I made arrangements to travel alone for several months on pilgrimage, fear sent me lovely memos that made me doubt what I was doing—memos like "You are bleeping crazy"; "You'll get lost, hurt, or killed"; "A pilgrim is categorically unemployable." But for some reason the real hook was the fear that this pilgrimage was just plain selfish, that I was deviating from my intended path of service. I often felt terrified and immensely uncertain of the choice I was making.

But I knew one thing unequivocally. I knew that this incendiary voice in my journal was the voice of love—the love that kneed me. I didn't know what I would have to meet; I didn't know where I would have to go. I just knew that I desired the feelings that the word *beloved* evoked in me and that I had to trust and acknowledge that desire.

I knew I wanted to move the way love wanted me to move.

What You Take with You

I used to think that the traumatic or trying events in my life were a seven-piece luggage set that traveled with me wherever I went. That perspective weighed me down, slowed me down, and made me feel as if my soul had a Wide Load sign attached to it, like those flatbed trucks taking up two lanes on the highway while transporting a mobile home.

Here's where a veil lifts.

In my experience, there is a story the ego is telling me about who I am and what is happening in my life that is filled with fear. And the voice of fear is usually loud and very close—right all up in my face. And then there's another story that the voice of the soul is ceaselessly recounting to me beneath all that surface noise.

These two stories are told in two different kinds of time: *chronos* and *kairos*.

Chronos, or chronological time, is linear, sequential "clock time": this is where the ego lives and thrives. We often want time to unfold in this way, one event following the next and arriving just when we want it to arrive. Kairos, on the other hand, is nonlinear, sacred time— the right or opportune moment.

We can pray our butts off for something to happen, say finding a lover, or getting a car or house, or having a long-awaited child. But then the person we meet ends up smothering us with love we weren't ready for, or the car payments put us in debt and the house catches on fire, or the baby of our dreams has colic and we don't sleep for two years straight. Then we realize that maybe, just maybe, in willfully pursuing our ego's desire, we tampered with sacred timing. Kairos is aligned with the highest truth for our lives, and being aligned with kairos means not always getting what we want when we want it.

Kairos is the sacred time needed for us to meet with not only what fulfills us but also what fulfills a need in the world. Kairos works on our soul's timing, not the laminated timetable the ego has set up for our life. Kairos–time allows things to unfold naturally; nothing is forced or contrived into being out of fear.

When we judge where we are in our lives and how much we've achieved, we do so from a place of chronos. Our judgments are based on expectations we set for ourselves: job by 25; married with children by 30; book published by 35; own business by 40, and so on to the grave. Many of us measure ourselves by these milestones without even examining them to see if they're our own. Meaning some of these linear expectations are acquired through social osmosis. What shifts the weight of our baggage is simply *choosing* it. Owning the baggage as the particular story our soul needed to live out allows us to claim it. And oddly enough, claiming it allows us to then let it go.

Once we let go of some of the stories that have been defining and confining us, we can align our identity with a deeper truth—with the soul-story beneath the surface drama of who we are according to the ego. We can dive beneath the wreck we fear we've made of our lives to hear the story our soul is living out. Listening to our soul-story allows us to release the idea that life is something happening *to* us. We can claim the power to become the author of our own narrative.

This is how we begin, how we remove a crucial veil: we claim our baggage as the story of our soul. No matter how old you are or what you've been through, you can change your perception of what's possible by claiming what has weighed you down and what you've used as an excuse to remain closed and unworthy of love, and accept that your baggage is, in fact, your personal soul-story, which has unfolded in exactly the sacred time it required. You may not be where you wanted or expected to be at this point in your life, but you can choose to acknowledge that you are right where you need to be.

This does not mean that where you are is not painful or frustrating. But it does mean that you have the power to change your life in an instant, simply by changing your perspective.

Take all those stories you've used as a reason to not love yourself. It's time to see them as lessons to challenge, refine, and even polish your soul. You look at those hard-to-let-go-of stories, and you love yourself enough to see that you deserve much more than to dwell on them and punish yourself with regret. You own the stories that have kept you in hiding, knowing that they form the unique narrative of your soul. You also know, however, that they are only a part of your journey, not the whole.

In this way you clean out your inner closets. You dig out the piles stashed behind the couch and under the bed, in the basement, the attic, and the spare room, and you lay the contents of your life at your feet. You sift through everything that makes up who you are and what you will be able to do and become.

If we didn't have baggage, if we didn't have dark, troubling stories in our lives, how would we ever get to practice the power of our love? What if every traumatic event we've endured, every regretful choice we've made, is actually an opportunity for the soul to spread its wings? We lift the weight of what has held us down by choosing to believe that everything in our lives has happened for our soul's formation. It has not only happened for a reason but happened exactly when it needed to. And that means births and deaths, marriages and divorces, epic gains and epic losses.

At the end of the movie *Ghost,* Patrick Swayze's character, Sam, is about to enter the infamous "light." As he kisses his wife (played by Demi Moore) with his translucent soul-lips, he tells her, "It's amazing, Molly. The love inside, you take it with you."

This is when I always do the ugly cry—not out of sadness but out of the pure joy that comes from recognizing the truth. This scene reminds me with such clarity and simplicity that there is really only one thing of importance in my life—cultivating the capacity to love.

Imagine putting down all that baggage you've been dragging around and then filling a tote bag, a little red one, with love. Imagine traveling with just that—and nothing else—wherever you go.

What you take with you now is entirely up to you.

The Second Veil

REVEAL Your Sacred Body

*Here in this body are the sacred rivers, here are the
sun and moon, as well as the pilgrimage places. I
have not encountered another temple as blissful as
my own body.*

— Saraha Doha

Body and Soul

You remember her. She looks just like you. She has
fire in her eyes. She is filled with adventure. She loves
without conditions and without boundaries. And her
presence is so fierce simply because she is unafraid in
her own skin.

She's just a little girl. She's the little girl you were
before some event or series of events separated you from
her. She's you before you began to fear her vulnerability,
her fragility, her wild and wide-open heart. She's you

before you forgot that she's the most powerful aspect of you.

Let me describe a picture I have of my fiery little irreverent girl-self. I'm seven or eight, pre-boobs, an intensely physical and uninhibited creature. This is clear at first glance. I'm at the beach with the ocean behind me. My hair is stiff with dried seawater and wild looking. I clearly don't care. I have my swimsuit yanked down in front to about mid-body, with my hip thrust out to one side and a crazy wide smile across my face. My soul is flush to my skin like a comforter is to a duvet cover.

This is the wild girl-child, the fully embodied beauty I was before my friend's older brother sexually abused me, before I let fear settle into my bones, creating a distance and a disconnect between my body and my soul.

I held on to this picture over the years, mostly because it was proof that there was a time when I walked unafraid in my own skin. There was a time when I felt safe to be fully who I am without taming, toning down, or denying the fiery soul I have inside me.

APOSTACY

The first time I read the Bible, I broke out in hives. My skin always broadcasts what's true for me, my emotion announcing itself across my face and down my neck. (Poker has never been my game.)

Let's begin with this: I'm ten years old, sitting in the basement of the First Unitarian Church of Cleveland for what will be my last day of Sunday School—ever. The parent-teacher-man—who is conducting the class—explains to us that the Bible or Old Testament, which we each have a copy of in our hands, is considered God's word by the majority of Jews, Christians, and Muslims. God's word. I couldn't get the idea out of my head. God writes? God has published a book?

Then we move on to the story of Hagar and Sarah. We each take turns reading about Hagar, a slave, and Sarah, Abraham's wife. Sarah was not able to conceive, which was her obligation as a wife in those days. Since Hagar was enslaved, she was forced to be the childbearer for Sarah and her husband. But then Sarah conceived at last. So Sarah threw Hagar out of the house, into the wilderness, along with her child.

This is when my skin went from mild protest to total rebellion. As we read through the description of the ways in which these two women were treated and how they related to each other, I became enraged. I pushed myself back from the table. I flipped ahead a few chapters, and then I flipped back. Wherever I looked I saw that the stories were the same. They were *about* women, but we didn't hear from these women in their own voices.

I tried to figure out how to say something, how to interrupt this gentle teacher-man's lesson, but my skin had that covered for me. I was a mini-Gorbachev by this point: my forehead had that same blood red blotch as if the boot of Italy had been stamped on my face.

And then the teacher asked me for my thoughts, even though I hadn't managed to raise my hand. I stammered out something like, "We don't know what it was really like for them, for the women."

I tried to say more but my ten-year-old intellect didn't know how to articulate what my body seemed to understand with ease—the truth that something terrifically crucial was missing here. In that moment, I felt my frustration ignite like a cloth doused in gasoline meeting an open flame. I was lit with an anger I had no idea what to do with. So I pushed my chair back from the table, stood up, slammed the Holy Book of God's Word shut, and did what I knew how to do: I marched dramatically out of the room.

In fact, I marched all the way out of the church. Then I sat down on the curb in the church parking lot and tried to figure out why I was so angry. All it took was that single moment of reflection, and I knew. It wasn't anger: it was fear. Pure fear. I felt more afraid than I had ever been. I wrapped my arms around my knees and started to sob.

I have returned to that moment throughout my life because it left singe marks on my soul. It branded me. It shaped who I was to become. I know now that I was so terrified in that moment because my sexual assault no longer felt random. Unconsciously, a connection had been made. My silence about what had happened that night with my friend's brother and his wrongful belief that he had a right to my body had everything to do with the fact that "God's word" had left women's voices out of the story.

As a little girl, this knowing was only visceral. I knew, as if in blood memory, that the female body, including mine, had been written out of the Divine equation. In that moment, sobbing on the curb in the church parking lot, I was terrified because I was female. I was the sex not considered sacred.

If my body contained a door, that door would be in my heart. And if I could describe that moment to you at all, I would say that I opened the door in my heart just then and walked right out. Apostasy is the act of abandoning one's religious tradition or faith. For me, though, the real apostasy that day was not leaving the church or my faith but abandoning my own body.

UNBREAKABLE HOLINESS

The first time I visited the Metropolitan Museum of Art in New York City I was 13 and obsessed with unicorns. The medieval tapestry of a captured unicorn, part of a series usually housed in the Met's medieval collection at The Cloisters uptown, happened to be on exhibit at the main museum. I stood before it mesmerized. Once my family and the other museumgoers had moved on, I inched closer. I wanted to be alone with the unicorn. I waited, captivated, as if expecting it to whisper to me.

I examined the threads that made up the fence, forming a perfect, luminous circle around the unicorn. There wasn't a gate or a single bent rail in the fence through which the unicorn could escape. It was trapped, yet it appeared entirely content. Had it been waiting to be released for a long time? Perhaps, I reasoned, it had finally given up.

Then it hit me. Maybe the function of the fence was not to entrap the unicorn but rather to keep the world from entering its space. Maybe the fence was the unicorn's protection. Slowly I began to recognize why I was so entranced by this tapestry. To me, the unicorn was an emblem of self-possession. It stared out with such confidence, such a sense of self-worth, as if the fence was merely a symbol of its inherent numinosity.

As I stared at the unicorn, I started to shake from the effort of trying not to cry. At 13, I didn't understand why the self-proclaimed sacredness I saw in this tapestry moved me so much. My feelings confused me. But I know I felt hope—hope that such a protected, coveted place could exist in me; hope that one day, like the unicorn, I could look out at the world from a sacred, inviolable place in my own body and unshakably know my own worth.

That moment reminded me of a crucial something that I knew could never be taken from me. I had no name for it at the time, but I know it now as my body's unbreakable holiness. The image of the unicorn intimated that there is an eternal, unconditional aspect within each of us, a secret garden that no one else can touch. It has a hidden latch that only we have the power to open. And it's there waiting within us, like a neglected oasis visited too infrequently or not at all.

A More Meaty Mary

I would always hesitate before opening the door to St. Elizabeth's Infant Hospital because once inside, the rest of the world would cease to exist. Nothing else could compete with the presence I met once I entered. St. E's, a Catholic Charities organization in San Francisco, was a place of mother's milk and indigestible pain, a place for the excluded—the controversial population of pregnant teens and teen moms.

An icon of the Virgin Mary was perched on top of the refrigerator in the staff lounge. Her four-foot plastic frame was so light that she teetered every time a child-care counselor or Sister of Charity opened the refrigerator door to retrieve their lunch from inside.

She was the "classic Virgin," I was told—the Mary most readily found in small enclaves in places of worship, especially in stone grottos on the periphery of church grounds. Her solemnity was expressed in her downcast eyes, her pursed lips, and her white hands pressed tightly beneath her chin in prayer.

It irritated and intrigued me to see Mary so easily jostled. I would shoot a frustrated glance her way every time I caught her teetering back and forth, as if to ask in exasperation, "How did we let you become so ethereal?"

It took approximately three minutes to ascend the stairs that separated the staff lounge from the floor where the teenage clients of St. E's Parenting Program resided. I walked up those stairs slowly, savoring the silence and the light. Once I stepped onto the linoleum tiles of the third floor, the raw intensity I met with demanded every ounce of me.

The smell in the corridor of the third floor was a potent mix of cocoa butter, baby formula, and disinfectant. The sounds of babies crying and music blaring blended in an unsettling cacophony of too much seriousness too soon, real life interrupting youth.

All the teens etched themselves into my heart, but one in particular struck a match up against it and lit it on fire. She had been raped and then thrown out of her mother's house for being pregnant. After spending several nights in jail for prostitution, she was sent to St. E's.

One morning, I was there when she found herself suddenly very vulnerable and afraid, as the reality of the imminent birth finally hit her. She turned to me and on this rare occasion actually looked me in the eyes and said, "I could use some God right about now."

I started to ask about her religious or spiritual background, but she stopped me with a quick flick of her hand and said, "Find me a more meaty Mary, then we'll talk."

My jaw dropped. Her honesty stunned me. I looked at her in awe. The recognition in her quick, sideways glance at me was electric. We both smiled, as if suddenly and if only for that second, we were on the same sacred team.

That was it. She had named it: a more meaty Mary. We needed an embodied Mary. We needed images and stories of the Divine Feminine that affirm the sacredness of the female body, images and stories of a Divine Feminine that can carry the weight of the darkness as well as the light.

How could these teenagers, some as young as 13, be reminded that they are sacred, that their bodies are holy regardless of rape, incest, and prostitution? Would these girls even be in this situation if the female body was revered as holy in the major world religions?

Where had Mary's body gone?

At that time I didn't identify with the more traditional religious sense of "being called." So I won't tell you I was called to go on the group pilgrimage to the Divine Feminine the summer before entering divinity school. The truth was far more ordinary. It was simply too painful to stay still, to see these teenaged girls who were so uncared for materially and spiritually. And it was especially painful to see that these young girls, with names I will never forget, cared so little about their own bodies. Because I was right there with them: I had no idea how to love my body or even be in it.

There's a story in an ancient Hindu text, the *Mahabharata*, about the goddess Kali's birth. All the male gods have gotten together in a godlike conference call, and they're freaked out because the world is completely out of balance. The demons, or *asuras,* are running rampant. And the male gods, despite all their efforts, realize that they cannot defeat the demons on their own. Though they had created this imbalance, they could not correct it. So the male gods agree that their only chance of survival is to collectively call for Kali to come into being so she can clean up their mess. They needed the fiercest form of the Divine Feminine to come in savior-style and defeat the demons.

So Kali is born out of the forehead (or the consciousness) of the goddess Durga. (Durga is also a great warrior goddess—just not quite as fierce as the sword-swinging, skull-wearing Kali Ma.) Kali comes barreling out of Durga's forehead and with a kick-ass sharp sword slays the demons, which represent the false beliefs created by the imbalance between the masculine and the feminine— beliefs like the one that says it's okay to tolerate rape and violence against women and girls. Kali sweeps in and chops all those false beliefs to bits, and peace is restored because the fierce Divine Feminine has brought the masculine back into balance.

I knew as I witnessed and worked with the teenaged mothers at St. E's that this is where we were as a world culture. We were at the point in the *Mahabharata* when the male gods sound a unified cry for the fierce Divine Feminine to rise.

I heard the call.

NOTRE DAME DE VASSIVIÈRE

I had seen the Black Madonnas of Chartres, Marsat, Clermont-Ferrand, and Le Puy with China Galland and a bevy of women mostly 30 years my senior. And now we were nestled in the mountains of central France, in the small medieval town of Besse to see the Black Madonna named Notre Dame de Vassivière.

As we gathered in front of the enormous wooden doors of the Saint-André church, China went over some history associated with this particular Black Madonna. She may date back to around 1805, possibly as a replacement for a statue of the Black Madonna destroyed by fire in the French Revolution. Often described as being crudely carved, Vassivière is known as the least majestic of all the Black Madonnas. The icon itself is a reliquary—a container for sacred relics like the physical remains of a saint. She has a door in her back, but the relics she contains are unknown.

Marion Woodman, a Jungian analyst and mythopoetic author, describes the ideological dimension of the Black Madonna as "nature impregnated by spirit," which is practiced or lived out by "accepting the human body as the chalice of the spirit."[1] According to Woodman, the Black Madonna is emblematic of the redemption of matter, of the illumined intersection of sexuality and spirituality.[2]

The Black Madonna is black not just because of her relation to the Egyptian goddess Isis but also because "she has literally or figuratively been through the fire and has emerged with an immense capacity for love and understanding."[3]

Woodman articulates the alchemical process that the Black Madonna seems to inspire or perhaps demand of her pilgrims:

> The pain of the transformation is real—physically and psychically—but only the intensity of the fire can unite body and soul. This is a soul-making process. That it is so is seen not at the

beginning but at the end. The body is the grit that produces the pearl.[4]

For this reason, Woodman claims the Black Madonna as "the patron saint of abandoned daughters who rejoice in their outcast state and can use it to renew the world."[5]

As soon as we entered the church, I made a beeline for the Black Madonna. I moved unfalteringly past rows of wooden chairs and a stone partition as if I had always known precisely where to go to stand before her.

Her features were haunting, like those of the crone, the archetypal old woman who had come to me in dreams. Rough and unfinished, like an image still coming into focus, her face was what I thought Earth might look like if it took human form. Notre Dame de Vassivière was entirely new to me as an emblem of the sacred, and yet she was all too familiar as well.

Suddenly my skin started to feel warm and static-y, as if I had just pulled off a wool sweater in winter. And just as suddenly, I found myself on my knees, with my hands pressed tightly together, reaching out toward her form. The church was cold and the stone floor I was kneeling on was even colder, yet it felt as though my body had been lowered into a warm bath. An overwhelming calm swept over me—a calm I had never known before. All my muscles relaxed.

Then I felt something else. It is hard to explain but it was unmistakable: I felt my own love.

The love that was pouring out of me toward this dark reliquary seemed to ricochet off the glass box surrounding her and return to me. I felt love for the skinny girl down on her knees in the middle of a French church when her peers were back home in the States starting careers and families. Here she was—here I was—knees pressed to medieval stone, right where my soul had led me. My love encompassed what it never had before: all of me.

And while the feeling lasted, I knew that nothing extraordinary was happening. I was merely in my body and unafraid. It seemed natural, nothing astonishing or unusual. It was just the love innate to a soul remembered back into the body.

What remains most lucid is the confusion I felt once I resurfaced from the lovefest the Black Madonna had inspired. I wish I could have simply lit a candle beside her glass box and walked slowly from the church into the rain. But as it was, I came up as if from the bottom of a quiet, warm pool, to a surface where I could hardly get air, a surface swarming with all these other swimmers kicking and flailing about in the water, in a confused effort to try and help me swim, convinced that I had almost drowned.

China seemed to be the only one undaunted by what had happened to me. She was on her knees beside me, silent and smiling.

Once I could speak, I asked her in a whisper what the other ladies were doing. Some were calling out to Jesus; others were praying for the Holy Spirit to intervene, making frantic gestures in the air. China said very softly, "For some, joy is terrifying."

We left it at that.

The rest of the tour group kept calling what happened to me a "mystical experience." I didn't know what to think. Something unprecedented had happened. I had been held on my knees before the Black Madonna for a long time. But to me, it had passed in a matter of moments. This experience was so unlike what I had imagined a mystical experience to be that I didn't recognize it as one.

I had anticipated angel sightings, a sense of being lifted up or elevated, trumpets maybe, definitely bright lights, and possibly even a disembodied voice telling me the dictates of my life. I did not expect physical bliss. I did not expect to pulse with undiluted love. I did not expect to feel fully connected to a source of love that is at once within me and more than me.

I also did not expect this: it didn't last. I thought that when the *coup de foudre,* the lightning, struck and Divine Love was revealed to me, I would be healed. I would feel whole, instantly and permanently.

And at first I *was* elated. I could feel the immensity of the gift I had been given that day. I was glowing, radiant. *This is it,* I thought, *I'm transformed.* But when I woke up the next morning feeling like I'd been hit by a Mack truck, I realized with disappointment that the path of the Divine Feminine, of revealing the soul in the human body, is a process and not an instantaneous transformation.

As Saint Teresa of Avila explains in *Interior Castle,* "There are many ways of 'being' in a place."[6] And by a place she means a body. She envisioned an entire mansion within her, room after room, where she met with the numinous, where the unsayable secrets passed into her from behind "a closed door."

But for me back then, on that first pilgrimage, I barely inhabited my pinky toes, let alone my entire body. Except for those succulent moments while I was held in that love grasp before the Black Madonna, I was most often not in my body at all. My life was shrouded in a pervasive inability to know and to claim what I wanted. Worst of all, I felt spiritual because of it. I felt transcendent, above it all. I wasn't listening to what my body was constantly telling me—that it was my own love I needed most.

What was revealed to me that day with the Black Madonna of Vassivière was that the Divine for me was in the opposite direction from where I'd been told to look. Until then, I had seen the Divine as something outside of me, beyond me, something I had to reach out of myself to attain. But now I had discovered that finding the Divine meant going within. And going within did not mean going toward the light and into the spirit, as so many holy books and spiritual guides direct, but rather, and rather ironically, it meant going straight into the dark, straight into the depths of my own flesh.

THE QUEEN OF THE OUTSIDERS

The small seaside village of Saintes-Maries-de-la-Mer was inundated with a mass gathering of Romani from all over the continent. The Romani, or gypsies, have long claimed Saint Sarah, Sara-La-Kali, as their beloved patron saint, and their devotion to her could be seen in every crevice of the place.

China and I were thigh deep in the Mediterranean. We were waiting for a sighting of the four horsemen who ritually carry Saint Sarah from her crypt down to the sea during this annual festival at the end of May. We were holding tight to each other's hands since the throng of people had twice almost separated us. Standing on tippy toes, we looked as far to the left and right as we could, trying to ensure that we caught a glimpse of Saint Sarah entering the sea.

There were thousands of people pushing and singing, as they waited with an anxious desire for Saint
Sarah to break through the crowd. I looked down at my
legs as the water lapped about them. Each caress felt like
a blessing. And then the horses were upon us—literally.
The four horsemen had emerged from the crowd right
where China and I happened to be standing. China
lurched forward toward the carriage and, with my hand
still clutched tightly in hers, reached toward the icon of
Saint Sarah, bobbing along regally as the crowd began to
chant "Vive la Saint Sarah! Vive Sarah-La-Kali!"

"Touch Sarah's cape!" China yelled. The horses had
begun to turn around and begin their procession back
to the church, to return Saint Sarah to her underground
crypt. China wanted to make certain that I didn't miss
this chance to touch her. It's considered a great honor.
She lined us up, and just as Saint Sarah passed us, China
pulled my hand to meet the ruffled edges of the icon's
brightly colored capes and gowns.

The persuasive tide of the procession retreated back
toward shore, taking me along with it. I lost hold of China's hand, but I didn't notice right away. Dripping wet
from the seawater, I repeated the song the Romani were
singing as if it had been sung to me as a child, singing
with the heart I heard around me. I had joined them. We
were all outsiders and this Saint Sarah was our queen.

Soon we were all in the crypt, reinstalling her in her
corner among the candles and abandoned crutches and
other paraphernalia of the cured. I say *we,* but really it was
just the women. At some point, the men had stopped
filtering into the church, and only women came below,
only women tended to the saint, readjusting her capes
and gowns as if she were a real little girl.

I felt like any other woman down there, adoring her. But then a life-worn woman with a face like a road map took me by the shoulders and laughed hard into my eyes. At first I wasn't certain what to do. I thought she was laughing at me or singling me out as a foreigner. But then the other women joined in, so my only recourse was to laugh, too.

This seems to have been the right response, because the woman folded me in an embrace that held my whole being, not just my body. She adjusted the bandanna on her head and led me up to the saint. Demonstrating how to embrace Saint Sarah, she lifted several of the icon's gowns so she could place her hands directly on Saint Sarah's side. Then she pressed her left cheek to the right side of Saint Sarah's face and rubbed it forcefully back and forth. She then did the same to the opposite side of the icon's face. As she released the statue from her embrace, the old woman slid her thumb three times down the bridge of Saint Sarah's nose. All this explained why the paint was missing from the nose, as well as why the saint's cheeks were worn down to the original wood.

Turning toward me, the old woman took me by the shoulders and pushed me toward Sara-La-Kali with a smile. I approached the icon with all eyes on me. And in that moment I realized that I loved Saint Sarah more than any other icon we had seen on the pilgrimage. She wasn't encased in a glass box as most of the Black Madonna icons had been. Weathered by love, she was worn down to the proverbial bone like the rest of us. She was right here with us, not set above or set apart. She was on the same level we were, face to face.

As I approached the icon, I marveled at the women around me. With just one look at the longing on my face, these "gypsy" women, deemed outcasts by society, had enfolded me into their circle and let me love their saint as my own.

At first I think I overdid the embrace as if to prove to them just how much I adored and identified with the Queen of the Outsiders. But once I was near Saint Sarah, I sobered up. I suddenly felt alone with her. The saint's diminutive size made me think of her as a daughter. I whispered to her as I pressed my cheek to her cheek, just as the old woman had done. And then I ran my thumb along her nose, a gesture that felt as familiar as it did endearing. I stared at her for one last minute before the woman with the mapped face pulled me away to let another woman embrace the saint.

The taper candles were glowing straight and strong. The air in the crypt was heavy and still, it smelled of candle wax and an ancient wetness. I backed into the corner and watched as the women, one after the other, embraced Saint Sarah. The honoring of her small feminine form unraveled me. I leaned against the far wall and then slid down it until I was sitting. I closed my eyes as hot tears surfaced.

This adoration of the feminine as holy, so painfully absent from my life, was what I needed most for my own healing. The vulnerable little girl in me had been cast out as too fragile, too human, too emotional, too weak. Somehow I blamed her rather than my abuser for what had happened to me. She had been too innocent, too trusting. She had shone too brightly. I had cast her out as I sat awake the rest of that horrible night. Rather than his darkness, I had feared her light—my own light.

And as I crouched in a corner of that moldy crypt, with the Queen of the Outsiders before me, I knew that this was how I needed to honor the Divine Feminine within me every day for the rest of my life—with colored capes and a golden crown, with four horsemen parading her before a crowd singing her praises all the way down to an all-embracing sea.

MARY MAGDALENE'S EGG

A dark-skinned icon of Saint Mary Magdalene painted by the Franciscan friar Robert Lentz has watched over me since I returned from the first pilgrimage. She is the focal point of the wall opposite my bed—a wall that is covered with images of the Divine Feminine, including the Annunciation to the Virgin Mary, the Hindu saint Amma, Wisdom Sophia, and a small painting of Notre Dame de Vassivière that China gave me.

This particular icon of Mary Magdalene is wearing a blood red cape as supple as worn muslin, wrapped about her shoulders and head. She points with one hand to the luminescent egg she is holding in the other. A small leaflet taped to the back of the icon gives an interpretation of her story. It goes something like this: on Easter morning, Mary Magdalene was the first to witness Jesus's resurrection. The Eastern Orthodox tradition believes that after the Ascension, Mary traveled to Rome, where she was welcomed in the court of Tiberius Caesar because of her high social standing. She reported to him how poorly Pontius Pilate had handled Jesus's trial and how little justice had been served. And she told Tiberius that Jesus had risen from the dead. To help explain His resurrection, Mary picked up an egg from the feast set before them. Tiberius responded with disbelief and said that a human being could no more rise from the dead than the egg in her hand could turn red. The egg turned red immediately.

While I was in seminary, I wasn't shocked to discover that there is no historical evidence to support the contention that Mary Magdalene was a prostitute. Research by Harvard scholar and theologian Karen King reveals that Mary of Magdala who became known as the Magdalene was most likely one of the benefactresses of Jesus's ministry. In other words, Mary was Jesus's sugar mama. She was not the woman with seven demons who Jesus cured. This, King illuminates, was a contrived description created by the Catholic Church. The Catholic Church has even written a formal apology for defaming Mary's true identity, i.e., calling Mary a whore for over two millennia.

What *did* shock me, however, was learning that Mary Magdalene has her own gospel and that like the Eastern Orthodox story of the red egg, Mary's gospel intimates that she has a crucial message to teach us about the body. In my gut I have always known that Mary Magdalene was something far more heretical than a prostitute. And by the fifth verse of her gospel, which dates back to the early 2nd century, I understood why it is seldom studied or discussed in religious institutions. It is way too challenging to the status quo. In the Gospel of Mary Magdalene, a woman occupies a place of legitimate spiritual authority.

At one point in the gospel, the disciples are stressed out and upset, not knowing how they will be able to preach Jesus's teachings now that he has been crucified. "If they didn't spare him, how will they spare us?" they ask. Mary, in full spiritual prowess, addresses them as her brothers and basically tells them a 2nd-century version of "Pull it together," saying, "Do not weep and be distressed nor let your hearts be irresolute." She tells the disciples to focus on praising Jesus's greatness, reminding them that they should be grateful to him, "for he has prepared us and made us true human beings."[7]

With Mary cast as the predominant spiritual authority, her gospel makes it clear, Karen King asserts, that spiritual advancement must come from "transformation within a person"[8] and "that leadership is to be based upon spiritual achievement rather than on having a male body."[9]

According to a popular folk legend, after the Ascension, Mary Magdalene crossed the Mediterranean to the south of France with her daughter, known as Sarah the Egyptian. Traveling with Mary of Bethany and Mary Salome in a boat without sails, Mary Magdalene and Sarah landed in the small seaside village that came to be known as Saintes-Maries-de-la-Mer.

Through deeply immersing myself in Mary's gospel and her history and legend from a theological perspective, I left seminary convinced that the Magdalene was meant to be the voice of the body. She imparted a truth just by being female. Her presence in Jesus's ministry, I ardently believe, was intended to teach us all—but especially the early church fathers—that ultimate spiritual authority comes from the quality and depth of our spiritual transformation within. Whether we are male or female, the body does not delimit or devalue our spiritual potential.

Mary Magdalene's voice was the one I sensed was missing as a little girl long ago. Her message seems to have been buried not in an alabaster jar deep in the desert but rather here in a secret chamber behind my heart.

I remember her. We all do. When we dare to risk being fully human, fully immersed in the fires of love, we remember again the divinity of the feminine.

I may not be an official member of any church but damn was Jesus smart to leave such a spiritual legacy in the form of a woman. It takes getting over the fact that she was female in order to receive it.

I Loved Her Fiercely

Before you can hear, much less follow, the voice of your soul, you have to win back your body. You have to go on a pilgrimage beneath the skin.

Here's what I've come to tell you: *Nothing good can ever be lost.*

No matter what has happened to you, there is hope. Even if you have only one memory, one image of what it felt like to be embodied—what it felt like before you became self-conscious, inhibited, or ashamed—there is hope. No matter how far away you are from your own body, no matter how distant that sacred, soul-filled little girl you once were seems to you now, she is still within you. She is waiting to be found.

Contrary to everything you've been taught, *she* is your knight in shining armor, the one you've been waiting for. She is what will save you, not that next job or that next love, not marriage, a child, or a trip to a tropical isle. What you long for most you already contain.

The most essential pilgrimage for you to make in this lifetime is to the place within that allows you to receive yourself—to be fully embodied and able to say, as the poet Ntozake Shange wrote, "i found god in myself / & i loved her / i loved her fiercely."[10] The path of the

Divine Feminine asks a woman to quietly, triumphantly turn within and, as Marion Woodman relates, "to be in love with her body . . . from the soles of her feet to the top of her head."[11]

I remember her. I have remembered my body's innate sacredness, and in doing so I allow my soul to return to its rightful place beneath my skin. I lift a veil between me and the Divine every time I claim my body as sacred by daring to come home to it again and again. Being at home in my body means having the courage to never discount or abandon the truth of my physical experience. It means listening when my body is speaking and having the audacity to voice the wisdom it contains. And it means acknowledging without reservation that the female body is the matter of an unbreakable holiness.

The Third Veil

REVEAL Your Soul-Voice

The Soul selects her own Society —
Then — shuts the Door —

—EMILY DICKINSON

IT COMES DOWN TO THIS

There comes a time in your life when the love you thought would never leave you does.

Maybe more than one person leaves you or betrays you. Maybe you even betray yourself. Maybe all the love you have received from outside of you suddenly pulls away. Or maybe it shifts slowly from you over the course of several years, so that you wake up one day almost astonished to find that there is seemingly no love surrounding you. And so at last you have the opportunity to come face to face with your own loving.

If no one else is doing the loving for you, you get a rare glimpse of the true source of all of your deepest hurts, desires, and dreams: your own love. You get to see if your inner well is bone dry or stocked to overflowing like those champagne pyramids with the bubbly cascading down on all sides.

There will come a time when the voice of your truth is the only voice you can hear because all the others have led you away from yourself. This voice of truth within you is the voice of your own beloved soul. It is the voice of unconditional love within you, the one you have no doubt denied or ignored or been too scared to hear, much less follow. Fear is normal, expected. But only love is real.

In those moments when fear eclipses what we want most for our lives, it is crucial to be able to connect to the still, calm voice that has a tight grasp on our greatest potential. It takes discipline, spiritual sweat, and Divine pluck to connect to the unassuming voice of the truth inside us. It takes audacity and courage.

This is such a crucial veil to lift. Are you loving *you?* Are you hearing the voice of love within you, your soul-voice, and believing it enough to act on its directives? This is what the practice of loving ourselves looks like: we do whatever we have to do to hear our soul's voice and believe it. We believe it so much that we make our life about that encounter.

FLIGHT 101 ON U.S. SCARE

My fear of flying began on a short flight I took with my older sister when I was 19. I was on my way back to college in Northampton, Massachusetts, after spending

Christmas in Cleveland with my family. It was a stormy night, but I didn't think anything of it. I felt safe in the air.

Arrival was a given since it was the flip side of departure. It never even entered my mind that I could leave from point A and never reach point B or that I might not make the return trip to point A as the same person. I won't say the name of the airline, since it could have been any airline, and the point of the flight wasn't to terrify me. I know that now. It was to free me. So, let's just call it Flight 101 on U.S. Scare.

I boarded U.S. Scare unafraid. But I would also say that I boarded it asleep. At that point my soul seldom looked out from behind my eyes. And I wasn't yet awake to this fact or to the tremendous impact it had on the quality of my life. All that changed, though, in a matter of an hour.

From the second we took off, our new normal became a horrific rattling of the cabin. I felt seat-buckled into the belly of some mechanical whale with tuberculosis; hacking coughs jostled its rib cage at unrelenting intervals. I held as tightly as I could to the armrests, as the bottom kept dropping out from beneath me. Whoosh, the plane would sink and then rattle furiously, sink and rattle. I wanted off. I wanted off in a way I had never experienced in my life. I felt like a trapped animal. But there was no ejector button, no escape route, no parachute. The only way out was through.

As the plane bobbed and dipped through the wild winter storm, somehow the well-put-together woman sitting in the aisle seat next to me was still managing to highlight sentences in her big spiral binder. The neon yellow ink veered off the page whenever the plane dropped suddenly, leaving wavy lines that looked like

the EKG of someone having an extreme myocardial in-
farction. Her calm only heightened my anxiety.

And so did my older sister's. She was sitting rock still,
staring out the window, when she wasn't reassuring me
that everything was going to be fine, that planes were
meant to withstand this kind of weather, that I could let
go of the armrests, that I could trust we were going to
land. Her every word was like oil hitting water. Not a bit
of reassurance permeated. I only knew fear. Fear was as
loud as the roar of the engines; fear was the only thing
I could hear.

How could the pilot risk our lives flying through this
crazy storm without even addressing us? This is what I
kept asking my sister. I knew taking a vote to see who
wanted to make an immediate U-turn was probably out
of the question, but I would have deeply appreciated
even just the smallest acknowledgment from the man at
the helm that he knew what the *bleep* he was doing. No
such announcement ever came.

I might as well sum it up by saying that I felt utterly,
completely, and entirely out of control. Aside from my
deathlike grip on the armrests, I was also digging my
heels into the floor of the plane as if I could somehow
slow it down. All I could do to try to calm myself was
imagine how grateful I would be to land. I imagined the
flood of love I would feel for everyone I laid eyes on,
everyone I spoke to, everyone I encountered even for
a moment. I imagined that transitional step from the
plane onto the gangway. I imagined the feel of sturdy,
solid earth beneath my feet. I imagined the smells of the
airport, the whirl of people careening toward their gates,
toward home. I imagined never being able to take even
the smallest detail of life for granted ever again.

I just wanted to be given the chance to love my life in a way that had not been possible for me before Flight U.S. Scare. I had pretended to be someone I wasn't without realizing it. Most of the time I was who others wanted me to be, at the expense of being myself.

I just wanted a second chance.

WHEN NOBODY AND NOTHING ELSE IS

I would recognize him again even if he were a zebra in a sea of other zebras. I only met him that one time, that one night, but I will never forget his smile, with that gap between his front teeth, a whole tooth wide. To save my life I can't remember his name, although probably that's because I made up mine when we finally shook hands. He was leaning against his cab like an urban cowboy, his hat tilted slightly forward, his feet crossed confidently at the ankles. Let's call him the Lone Ranger, so it's easier for us to remember that this isn't his real name.

I was wheeling my carry-on behind me, and fear was radiating from every pore of my body. I had watched my older sister board our connecting flight, but there was no possible way I was going to trust my now-precious, never-to-be-taken-for-granted-again life to the indelicacies of metal hurling itself through the air at such hubris-filled heights. I waved good-bye to my sister and opted to stay with a friend outside of Philadelphia, where we had landed, and take a train to my college the next day.

Once I moved over far enough to get my suitcase in the cab beside me, the Lone Ranger closed the door. The leather of the backseat was cracked and worn. I noticed the cross dangling from the rearview mirror immediately. I could tell it was a good cross. Some crosses scream at me as soon as I see them. They are about hell and damnation, fire and brimstone—all the glorious trappings of judgment and guilt. This cross didn't need me to believe for it to be real and true. This was a different kind of cross. For me, it represented a kind of crucifixion of the ego.

"So where are we headed?" the Lone Ranger asked, as he looked at me through the rearview mirror and smiled.

"Ardmore, I think it's called," I said in a hoarse voice that was deeper than normal from all the tension in my body after the flight.

"So we're headed to Haverford College, right?" he asked.

"Right."

"I've never been," the Ranger said, which probably should have concerned me. But then he added, "I know the direction we should go. I've got a map, and I'm not afraid to use it."

"Good enough for me," I said, as he pulled away from the airport, the taxi stand, the place of my real departure.

I know there was small talk for a while, but I can't recall the details. We commented on the usual things— the storm, the holidays, the fact that I was visiting a friend, that I had never been to Philly before, that I was a stranger in a place where he had lived his entire life. So my next question didn't come out of nowhere; we had at least covered the basics as we headed toward the suburb where my friend's college was located.

"Do you believe in God?" I asked him. When he didn't answer right away, I plunged into the details of the flight I had just gone through and how grateful I was to be alive. I told him how terrified I felt on the plane and how I couldn't understand how everyone else acted as if nothing extraordinary had happened.

"It feels like I've survived a crash," I remember telling him, "even though we ended up landing safely. It feels like I went through death but then lived."

As I was speaking, we had taken an exit and were now stopped at a light. The Lone Ranger smiled again, first in the rearview mirror, and then he took this chance to turn around and blast me full on with the widest possible smile his face could manage. Without retracting the width of his smile in the slightest, he said, "Hate to be the one to have to tell you this, but you're still on that airplane now."

When my eyebrows shot up to my hairline, the Ranger laughed and asked, "Who do you think is driving this cab?"

The answer "You are" popped into my head but was far too obvious to be right. So I sat in silence. The Ranger pulled over at a deserted Gulf station and left me in the car to ruminate on an answer while he unfurled his map on the hood of the cab. I watched as he held down the corners of the map in the freezing wind, and marveled that he was willing to go through all this to get me where I needed to go.

"We're getting closer," he said as he pulled the door shut and slid the dial on the heater from low to high. The cross swayed as we caught the edge of the sidewalk while turning onto the street.

"I know the answer's God," I said, frustrated. "But I have no idea what that means. I mean, where was God tonight when for a solid hour I was terrified and positive that I was going to die feeling like I had only half-lived what little of my life I've had so far?"

Again, the Lone Ranger smiled. But this time to himself, facing forward, eyes on the road. I didn't need for him to direct his smile into the rearview mirror. By that point, I could feel his smile when it came. It was like the presence of something larger than either one of us, and it filled the whole cab with a profound silence that forced me to hear the unfaltering and raucous beat of my own heart at work.

"We're all on an airplane," he said, "all the time." I knew he would continue so I didn't say anything and waited. "You don't fear being in this car with me because you can see that I'm at the wheel. You can fool yourself into believing that I'm in control. But I'm not."

I'm pretty sure I folded my arms or looked out the window at this point. He noticed my resistance.

"I'm going to tell you a story about a good friend of mine," he started, the smile still with us. "Now, this friend went through a long, drawn out time of losing his wife because he drank too much after work, losing his job because he had lost his wife, and then losing his house because he had lost his job. He became a cabbie, like me, and got through each day, just barely. He felt alone. And feeling alone made him want to drink. So there he was late one night, coming back from a bar as drunk as he was black, speeding like he meant for the car to crash.

"To this day he can't figure out how it happened. But as he began to cross the bridge, he lost control of the car. It flipped over once before crashing through the guardrail. The next thing he knew, the car was dangling from the edge of the bridge, hanging on as if by a fingernail.

He couldn't move. Any second the car might fall, and he had no idea what to do to save himself. And that's when he heard it."

"Heard what?" I interrupted, with inevitable curiosity.

"I guess you could say God. He heard God. But this is what hit him. God wasn't what he had thought. God wasn't a man or a woman. God wasn't black or white either. God's what's there when nothing and nobody else is."

The truth has always made goose flesh of my skin. All my tiny arm hairs were giving the Lone Ranger a standing ovation as soon as he said this.

We pulled onto the Haverford campus and wound our way through the well-marked paths to the main student hall, where my friend was waiting for me. I paid the Lone Ranger the fare and a large tip. I was so grateful that we were there and that he in particular had been behind the wheel.

"What's your name?" he asked as he opened the cab door and pulled out my suitcase. I was obsessed with mermaids at the time. I loved the metaphor they embodied: a woman who could be in two worlds at once. So I told him that my name was Madison, as in Daryl Hannah's character in the movie *Splash*.

He reached out his hand to me in the space between us and said, "Don't be afraid to fly, Madison."

Now it was my turn to smile. "Tell your friend that he may have lost a lot, but he's a lucky man to have found the God inside him."

LIVING IN SIN

In the series of 13 concatenated nightmares I had in the months following Flight U.S. Scare, the only variation among them was in the passenger sitting next to me. I crashed with a woman who drooled and wore a sun visor that read Key West Is Where It's At. I crashed with an enormous man wearing an anorak and eating a bag of Cool Ranch Doritos. And I even crashed with the dream man himself, Carl Jung. He was smoking a pipe while the red No Smoking sign flashed above our heads.

I don't say prayers or rushed good-byes to my loved ones in the nightmares, as I would have expected, or as others are doing when each of the 13 planes plummets to Earth. For me, in this moment, there is no single name to grasp or cling to. There is no chant, mantra, or thought that can console me the way "Why me?" seemed to capture adequately the pain of Visor Lady, and "Jesus *bleep*-ing Christ" seemed to sum it up for Dorito-breath Man.

As the airplane's cabin convulses and collapses, and a baby wails with all her might, I watch with violent frustration because there was something I had wanted to say. There was someone I had wanted to be. I still had a tome's worth of love within me that I had never given away. In each of the nightmares, I realize too late that I had let fear keep me from being who I am. I had let fear silence me. And in these nightmares, silence was the same as having had nothing at all within me to share.

And that was the real nightmare. It wasn't just death I faced. It was something far worse. I had never revealed my soul.

The most common definition of the word *sin* is "a deliberate transgression of religious or moral law." When it comes to theology, sin is most often understood as either deliberate disobedience of the will of God or a condition of estrangement from God as a result of disobedience. I've always kept my distance from this definition of sin. Actually, you'll never hear the word *sin* leave my lips. I don't find it useful, mostly because I've witnessed people use it to judge others, rather than to help understand and refine their own actions.

The texts that make up the New Testament were originally written in Greek. The Greek word *hamartia* (ἁμαρτία) is usually translated as sin. But in Greek, it doesn't mean to commit a moral or religious transgression. Sin simply means "to miss the mark," or "to miss the target."

If sin is simply missing the mark, then what comes to mind is the red bull's-eye. Alignment with Divine will would be the opposite of sin. Imagine that the red bull's-eye is simply Divine Love. Imagine that being in love and acting from that love is all that the Divine wills for our lives. Lack of distance then from that unconditional love would be alignment, a bull's-eye. And likewise, distance from love or disassociation from the reality of love would be "missing the mark."

The nightmares were not trying to make me even more terrified of flying, though they did for over a decade. The nightmares were meant to show me what sin means in my own life. My plane kept crash-landing, falling short of the mark or target, because I kept allowing fear to dictate my life.

Fear kept the real me locked deep inside.

I BELIEVE I CAN FLY

The summer after graduating from college, right before I moved across country to San Francisco, I volunteered at a shelter in Cleveland that housed children as they awaited placement in foster homes.

That's where I met India. She was rail thin but as sinewy as a prizefighter, with a surprisingly deep voice. The contradiction of such a low, manly voice in this tiny twig of a girl was endearing. I could always hear her coming from way down the hall. Her braided hair had colored beads that clicked against each other when she moved, which she never stopped doing. India was the most animated child I have ever met.

She was always telling a story or singing a song. And her favorite song to sing, especially while pumping her toothpick legs to propel her higher on the swing set out back, was one I hadn't heard before meeting her—a song I later learned was called "I Believe I Can Fly."

As a volunteer, I mostly read books to the children or listened to their outlandish stories and dreams. My days were spent playing make-believe. I usually didn't know their particular histories—the difficult circumstances that had landed them at the shelter.

One day I came into work, and India's fiery little animated spirit had literally gone mute. She was a shell of her former self. She looked at me when I spoke to her, but that radiant light in her eyes had gone out. Although she was physically there, in the most crucial way she was missing. It was devastating.

I learned that this was "normal" for India. She would "disappear." I was reassured that she always came back. But for days, sometimes weeks at a time, she fell utterly silent. One of the child-care counselors told me that this was because India had lost her mother. She had been in the same room when her mother's boyfriend had killed her. India's therapist was still working to uncover all that had happened that day. India had no known family who could take her in. I remember listening to her story as if I could handle it.

When the counselor finished, I excused myself to go to the bathroom. I locked the door and looked in the mirror. I saw the strain of trying not to cry in the lines on my forehead. But it wasn't the image of India having to witness her mother's death that made me sob; it was remembering the conviction I heard in her little voice as she soared through the air. I realized then that it was the presence of India's soul that held me rapt when she sang on the swing. She was using the voice of her soul to overcome her grief.

And even though it would seem to come and go, there was a tenacious presence of love in India, despite her trauma. I had witnessed it. Thanks to India, I remembered that there is a presence of love within us that no one and no circumstance can take from us.

THE CROSSING

The ship had not even left the Port of New York and I was terrified, as terrified as if I had just boarded a plane rather than the *QE2*. (Yep, the *QE2* as in the *Queen Elizabeth II,* the transatlantic ocean liner from back in the day.)

The same anxiety that would paralyze me just before takeoff and compel me to do whatever was needed to deplane—including lift a flight attendant twice my size—had me in its viselike hold even when I was "safe" aboard a ship. I stood in the humid September heat, on the threshold of the casino, which was the muster station I had been assigned to. The fire alarm was sounding, and all the passengers were participating in a compulsory fire drill before the ship sailed.

I was wearing a bright orange life preserver, which kept riding up underneath my chin. I had to hold it down with both hands to keep it on my chest and away from my throat. I was so stressed out that I began to doubt everything. Standing there with one foot in the hallway, one foot in the casino, and passengers in life preservers all around me, I started to sweat. The external noise sounded like a milder version of the five-alarm fire going on inside me.

Just then, I glanced over to the far right side of the casino. My eyes fixed on a kind-looking older man with pearls of sweat gathered across his forehead. His large glasses had lost their grip on his face and were sliding down the bridge of his nose. I smiled. Obviously he had followed the directions placed in our cabins more to the letter than anyone else. Underneath his life preserver, he had put on the several layers of clothing that were suggested should we have to disembark mid-ocean. He was blotting his forehead with a small handkerchief when our eyes met. Startled, I looked away.

His gaze suddenly made me conscious of how silly my stance must have seemed. I couldn't take that final step into the casino. I couldn't commit to this "crossing," as the stewards referred to it, and yet I also couldn't seem to leave. Every possible doubt had come to greet me. Why was I following through with this? Was I really going to travel across France to the shrines of the Black Madonna and Mary Magdalene on my own? Is there such a thing as a pilgrim in an H&M blouse and Seven Jeans?

I looked back at the older gentleman, seated at the craps table. He was patting the stool beside him. Something about the sincerity in his face set against the backdrop of the craps table—a tropical scene of palm trees and dangling bananas—made me smile and then relax. And once relaxed, clarity came. I had two choices. Walk toward this person and see what adventure this crossing had to offer me, or run like a madwoman for Aunt Mable's suitcase four floors below and then bolt for the nearest exit with the hope that all the gangplanks hadn't yet been pulled.

I walked toward the craps table.

As I crossed the casino floor, I thought of the prayer I had made before leaving the cabin, when I had first seen the tight quarters of the ship—an unromantic side to the crossing I had not anticipated. I had pulled out the poster of Anandamayi Ma I had brought with me.

Anandamayi Ma, or Joy-Permeated Mother, was a female Hindu saint born in the late 19th century. The poster is from an exhibit that Harvard hosted when a collection of her *bhajans,* or devotional songs to God, and short films about her life and teachings were donated to the divinity school library. For some reason, whenever I listened to her bhajans I cried. No, the word *cry* doesn't describe it. *Weep* is closer. I wept with my whole body. And I had no idea why. Something about the love in her voice and the way she sang each word (though I didn't understand her language) made me long for an experience of the Divine.

I put her image on one of the twin beds in my cabin and knelt beside it, praying for a sign that it was safe to stay on board. I was amazed at how headstrong and determined I had been to go on this pilgrimage, all because of a *yes* I got in red ink from the voice in my journal. And yet now I felt panicked and positive that I was just plain crazy. That was when the fire alarm went off.

By the time I was sitting on a stool beside the older gentleman, the ship's officer had begun to call for our attention. I resumed my struggles with the life jacket as I listened intently, concerned as I was about the rumors that we were headed straight out to sea and into a storm.

The officer demonstrated how to inflate our jackets further by pulling the cord on our shoulder and told us that the bulb on the other shoulder was saltwater sensitive and would light the moment we entered the ocean. I felt the precise anxiety I always felt when flight attendants pointed to the laminated instructions on what to do in the event of a crash.

Once the officer began answering the passengers' questions, the man beside me tugged at my elbow and whispered, "What's your name, little one?" He had a singsongy way of speaking, and when he finished, his head tilted to the left in a kind of sideways nod.

I leaned over, considered using Madison again, but said, "Megg."

"What's yours?" I asked, as the warmth of his presence began to reassure me.

"Anand," he said. My eyebrows raised in recognition.

"You know what this means?" he asked, surprised and entertained.

"Yes," I said with a wide smile. "*Anand* is Sanskrit for joy."

I told him then about my comparative studies of the Divine Feminine at Harvard. And since I was comfortable enough to tell him my real name, I also told him that

I was on a pilgrimage—an old-school, I-mean-spiritual-business, honest-to-goodness pilgrimage.

Joy listened, transfixed. By the time I had finished, his glasses had lost their hold on his nose. I nearly set them straight for him. As he started to tell me his story, he looked more like a 3-year-old child bursting with excitement than a 60-year-old man.

First, he told me that he was an architect by trade and that his single greatest influence and inspiration had been Le Corbusier, "the Raven." "There is a building on Harvard's campus that the Raven built," Joy explained, "one that contains his signature motif. There is a path that winds its way up through the many levels of the building. Doors open into different corridors that take you, willy nilly, all around the place. But there's one door that, if you find it, will take you on the path that leads straight through the heart of the building."

The fire alarm stopped. Joy and I slid from our stools as people began to file out of the casino and take off their life jackets. We agreed to meet on the Lido deck for a drink some night.

I knew that I had received the sign I prayed for—that Joy was my sign.

CAPE GRACE

From impressions left by black-and-white movies and episodes of *The Love Boat,* I thought the farewell would include confetti, champagne, and couples kissing. I imagined waving wildly to the crowds along the gangway. But the real departure was nothing like that.

As the ship was pulled into the harbor by a red tugboat at its stern, there were a few people blowing air-kisses from the pier, and a few passengers lining the deck, catching those air-kisses. It was all nice enough, if uneventful, yet I felt a sense of foreboding. But I couldn't understand it. Why would Tuesday, September 4, 2001, have any significance?

As we glided past the isle of Manhattan with its tall buildings on our port side, I was hit with an inescapable urge to race back down to the cabin for my camera. I had only one roll of film with me, not expecting to take many pictures, though I wanted to capture the view three days into the crossing when water is all you can see.

I ran to my cabin, grabbed my camera, and was back on deck just as we passed the iconic red umbrella on the Travelers Insurance Building. I snapped then snapped again, quickly, impetuously.

New York was here before me, a sudden lover, and I, only upon leaving it, realized that it wasn't an unrequited love. I began taking pictures as if kisses all across its skyline.

The picture I would come to treasure most was the last I was able to take before Manhattan receded too far from view and the ship was enveloped in thick fog. It is a picture of the island's southernmost tip, with the Twin Towers in the center of the frame.

Something pulled me as if from the back of my neck to the stern to keep my eyes on Manhattan for as long as possible. As I stepped up on the first rung of the back railing, a man nearby playfully tugged on my shirt and said, "One Rose Dawson is enough, already." I smiled ruefully and clasped the rail.

I stared at my knuckles, which had turned white with the strain of holding on so tight. The presence of so much fear frustrated me. I was so terrified of flying that I had signed up for nearly a week's trip across the Atlantic to avoid it, and yet the same full-bodied fear was here to greet me. If it wasn't just flying I was afraid of, what was it?

I wouldn't live into an answer for years, but that night I held a flashlight in my left hand and a red pen in my right. I was using the flashlight because I couldn't see the stars from my cabin's small porthole unless I turned off the lights. I listened to "Gabriel" by Lamb while reading my own handwriting, as if this voice that called me *beloved* was trying to tell me my own secrets. I wrote about the Alpha and Omega, about a T. S. Eliot poem I could only half remember that cryptically relates that the end will be where the beginning is, about the announcement the captain had made that the closest ship to us right now was Cape Grace, moored off the coast of Nova Scotia, and I wrote about the deep, near breathtaking desire I had to meet true love. And then I asked:

What do I need to know in this moment?

The answer I wrote:

love, true love, means no longer waiting.

The Messenger

I was not a practical pilgrim. Packing Aunt Mable's old hard-sided suitcase, I replaced a much-needed pair of sneakers with a pile of books, including Simone Weil's *Waiting for God,* Marion Woodman's *The Pregnant Virgin,* and Rilke's *On Love and Other Difficulties.* The suitcase I should have taken was a duffle on wheels, but Aunt Mabel's suitcase had a large monogrammed M on the top, near the handle. Having that letter M made me feel like I was part of a secret sisterhood of the Divine Feminine: M for the Madonna, M for the Magdalene, M for the Mother.

I also opted to leave out the extra "fancy" outfit the *QE2* had suggested I pack for the black- and white-tie dinners served nightly. Instead, I packed my portable altar, which contained the 18 x 24-inch glossy poster of Anandamayi Ma; a small but heavy icon of the Tibetan goddess Green Tara; a laminated saints card of Joan of Arc; the beads I got when I met Amma, the hugging saint; the icon of Saint Sarah-La-Kali from my first pilgrimage; and a piece of red cloth in honor of Mary Magdalene.

I only relate all these details to try to explain how I ended up sitting at the captain's table and meeting R. Kelly while not wearing any underwear.

Before dinner that night, when I put on the only nice skirt I had packed, I noticed with a shock that it rode lower in back than my thong strap. There was nothing else to do but go buck. I didn't realize it was the night that the captain would be dining with the passengers or, what's more, that he would be assigned to my table. Actually he was seated right next to me. Given the age of the average passenger—well into the golden years—I should have realized this was probably not a coincidence. But as self-conscious as I felt in my pantyless state, I loved meeting the captain. He was every bit a man of the sea, calm, quiet, serene, with a full, dark beard and eyebrows so thick they looked like two fuzzy wooly bears asleep on his forehead. He answered all my questions about the ship, which were mostly about the probability of it capsizing, as in *The Poseidon Adventure*. He found my fears humorous enough to push back from the table and slap his knee.

After dinner that night I was supposed to meet Joy on the Lido deck for a drink, but something led me trancelike into the ship's theater instead. *Shrek* was playing. I walked in at the part where Shrek takes off his helmet and reveals that he's an ogre, not quite the knight in shining armor that Princess Fiona had expected. She was supposed to be saved by a knight, not by this outcast green giant of a man with a donkey as his sidekick.

I glanced around at one point to see who else was in the theater. There was a row of men several rows behind me. Light reflected back at me from off their enormous diamond earrings.

I didn't want Joy to worry, so I stood up and left the theater to go meet him. But before I reached the stairs leading to the Lido deck, I heard a voice call out, "Hey, you there. Can I ask you something?"

I turned around and saw one of the diamond-studded men. In the light of the stairway I could see that he was wearing a black tee shirt with white lettering that read R. KELLY.

"Sure," I said, as I turned to face him.

"Do you know who R. Kelly is?"

"No," I said. "Sorry," I added, realizing that I didn't know the person he was wearing on his shirt.

"Yes, you do," he smiled. "You know 'I Believe I Can Fly.' That man."

Chills swept through me as I saw an image of little India on the swing set. "Yes, of course," I said, embarrassed.

"Well, he wants you to come back and watch the movie with us. Will you?"

For India's sake, I felt compelled to go. When I was actually standing in front of him, I lost it seven ways from Sunday. I could see that his lips were moving, but I couldn't hear him over my own anxious thoughts about what I should say. I doubt I made any sense. I know I mentioned India—how much his song meant to her—and I think for some reason my hands were in the prayer position for a second as if to salute him. Basically, I was a flustered mess.

When I finally arrived on the Lido deck, Joy gave me an exasperated look.

"I thought you had stood me up," he said, with his head tilting off to the side as if to punctuate his statement.

I apologized and then told him about India and why meeting R. Kelly had me dazed. When I finished, Joy started laughing and lifted his hand into the air to signal the waiter.

"This was a very important lesson for you to learn, little one," he said, somehow managing to be immensely serious while laughing so hard his belly jiggled beneath his canary-yellow Tommy Bahama shirt. "Never confuse the message with the messenger."

I got that message loud and clear the first day off the ship.

I was reading a celebrity column while lounging on my older sister's couch in Oxford, England. The article was about R. Kelly's arrival on the QE2. My sister came in with her gigantic tea mug and turned on the TV. I read on and learned that R. Kelly had mentored R & B queen Aaliyah and that the two had supposedly been illegally married. The column related with sad irony that ever since Aaliyah's death in a plane crash a month earlier, R. Kelly, famed singer of the hit song "I Believe I Can Fly," was afraid to fly.

My face flooded with emotion. I didn't know if it was true—if R. Kelly had been on the *QE2* for the same reason I was. It didn't matter. Meeting him reminded me of the realization I had when I met India, the one about the power of the soul to overcome the kind of suffering and paralysis that fear creates.

This was the article I looked up from when the TV show we were watching was suddenly interrupted with images of the Twin Towers. Dark smoke spiraled from the buildings, as commentators scrambled to understand what was happening.

THE DOOR IN MY HEART

I wasn't capable of seeing the visible layers of scaffolding that covered my real life until that moment. Everything that wasn't true to who I am, to what I had time for in my life, fell away. It took a very long time to fathom that the hijacked planes were not empty. I could only handle the truth in increments. I tried to ration the tragedy. I couldn't digest it all at once. But when I finally comprehended that those planes were commercial flights, I broke into irretrievable pieces. And this is when I heard it: the voice I had only ever met in my red ink surfaced from someplace inside me.

"Choose," it said.

The goddess Kali is known for severing the heads of her devotees. Sounds harsh, I know, but what it means symbolically is that she removes—forcefully, if she has to—the ego that often deludes us into thinking we are anything other than a part of the Divine. This is the best way for me to describe that moment. It was the moment when Kali beheaded me. I couldn't hide anymore or take directions from fear. Whack. This was it. I am a soul. This voice I have met in my red ink is the highest version of who I am, not someone or some power outside of me. As I met this face-to-face within, calm enveloped me, a calm I would come to recognize as the soul's footprint.

Suffused with this calm, I knew that the only thing I could ever really do for India or for the girls I loved at St. E's or for the lives that had been lost on 9/11 was to choose love in my own small life at all costs.

In *Eat, Pray, Love,* when Elizabeth Gilbert prays to God for direction, she gets an answer immediately. Yet, her answer comes not in a loud and booming, Old Testament–type voice. It comes in her own voice. But it's her voice as she has never heard it before, "perfectly wise, calm, and compassionate."[1] It's what her voice would sound like, she says, if she had only experienced love and certainty in her life. Rather than being a typical or traditional religious *conversion* experience, Gilbert understands this defining moment of hearing her own "omniscient interior voice"[2] as the beginning of a religious *conversation.* She goes on to travel to Italy, India, and Bali, but to me her journey really starts when she begins this Divine conversation. Instead of casting her prayers out to some Divine source above or beyond her, her prayers echo down into her core. The source of wisdom and unfaltering love is found deep within.

It takes most pilgrims years, a lifetime even, to get to this truth that Gilbert experiences before she even steps on a plane, tastes her first Italian treat, or meets the man she was meant to love. I refer to the voice I hear within me, the voice I recognized as my soul's own for the first time on 9/11, as the soul-voice.

I can recognize the soul-voice because it is most fierce when it comes to truth-telling, yet it never insists on its own way. The soul-voice will suggest I do that one thing I want least to do, not to annoy me but to get me to face fears, to grow, to change. The soul-voice, unlike the voice of the ego, is not about drama.

When Gilbert prays for God to tell her what to do, she expects to hear sublime advice about her imminent divorce, drastic changes she must make, or hard and fast lines she must draw in her love life. Instead, she hears a simple directive: "Go to bed, Liz." In that moment, this was the most sagacious, the most loving, the most compassionate advice she could receive. She just needed to take care of herself. The wisdom of what to do with her life, with matters of her heart, would follow without drama and without deadlines.

Every woman has to take the journey alone to meet her soul-voice and find the authentic truth that waits within her. Every journey taken is as different as the soul-voice found. But in my experience, the soul-voice is that one voice that is always and in all circumstances the voice of unconditional love. "Choose," I heard my own soul ask me. "Choose love even now."

Only Love is Real

In the past I have often been told that I'm too intense, I'm too much, or that I should "turn it down a notch." I've even been told that I'm more trouble than I'm worth. And I would respond by "smalling" myself, like a Slinky I would retract, shrinking back to half my soul's size. I would "tone it down" (or at least try to) and pretend to be far more of what others wanted, needed, and expected of me.

None of that is possible now. I can't dim or diminish who I am any more than a sea monkey that has met with water can squeeze back into its original packaging.

You will have to find the journey, pilgrimage, or spiritual practice that will forge a meeting with the soul-voice inside you. You will have to go through your own discernment process to distinguish the voice of fear from the voice of love.

The veil that lifts is this: there will never be a voice *outside* of you that is wiser than your soul-voice or holds more authority over what is best for you. You need guidance and support not to follow someone else's truth but to remain loyal to your own. The voice that will guide you to your highest potential is within you.

Why is this so important?

When we remember our own love, we know that it goes with us no matter what happens in our lives—no matter what pain or suffering we experience, or what fears, real or imagined. We have the love of our life right here within us, beaming a course for us to realize our potential and fulfill our deepest desires.

There will come a time when you can accept nothing less than the breathtaking truth of your soul, the voice of Divine Love within you.

The Fourth Veil

REVEAL Your Divine Worth

We are not held back by the love we didn't receive in the past, but by the love we're not extending in the present.

—Marianne Williamson

The Inheritance

This is the most important truth I have to tell you: *You do not deserve love.*

I know, it's a shocker. I remember the first time I heard it. My heart fell out of my chest. All color drained from my face. And the teacher-friend who told me this truth had to pick my jaw up off the table. I trusted him, though. So I worked through the initial slap to the soul that it felt like and really let it sink in.

And then the power of this truth transformed me. It redirected my thoughts, my actions. If I don't deserve love, I realized, then I also don't earn it. Love is innate. Love is inherent. Love is a birthright.

The teacher-friend who told me this truth loved me completely. And he saw me completely. I was human and also Divine in his eyes. I could be an animal with my passionate emotions and then in the same moment, an angel of wisdom and insight, which was not a contradiction for him. He loved all of me. Every piece was accepted.

At the time, I thought that I loved being in his presence because it was effortless to love myself when I was with him. The unconditional love he gave me was infectious. But I know now, after a decade of being apart, that his greatest gift was making me feel truly worthy. I loved to be with him because I saw my innate worth through his eyes.

I was beloved to him simply because I am.

This was the culmination of everything I had ever wanted. Meeting him—let's call him Will—was meeting with Divine Love in human form. And Will gave me the greatest possible soul assignment because he was not able to be with me as a life partner. So I had to learn how to look at myself as he had. I had to find myself beloved, worthy. I had to recover my own Divine worth from within.

LIVE AS ONE

Two newspaper articles from *The Guardian,* dated September 15, 2001, accompanied me on the train from London to Paris, my home base as I traveled to various pilgrimage sites of the Black Madonna and Mary Magdalene. I carried the articles folded and tucked in my back pocket, or in my journal, as a bookmark. I would touch them as if they could cast a net of reassurance, a calm when I lacked courage. When the train was midway beneath the English Channel and the two women across the aisle from me started conjecturing that a terrorist's bomb at these depths would drown us all, I unfolded the articles and read them again, the way some people turn to scripture.

The first article, "Silence, Sirens, Bells, and Lennon," is divided into sections under the bold-faced names of various European countries. The thread between them is a description of the reverence and remembrance each country showed for the people who died on September 11. All over Europe, for three minutes at noon on Friday, September 14, people stopped and observed a moment of silence. In squares, in markets, near churches, strangers stood together to bear witness to what had happened. The photo showed a large group of people with their heads bowed, holding hands.

The section on observances in France reads in part: "The stock exchange stopped trading, and Paris metro trains stood immobile as a short statement of sympathy was read over the loudspeakers. Some radio stations stopped broadcasting for a minute at noon, while others played John Lennon's 'Imagine.'"[1] I had just been to the John Lennon exhibit at the Rock and Roll Hall of Fame in Cleveland, a week before leaving for New York City to board the *QE2*.

Lennon's video of "Imagine" was playing nonstop in a small, dark theater on the second floor. I entered toward the end. As I sat down, Lennon was looking straight into the camera's lens. From behind an all-white piano in an all-white room, he was singing the last refrain. I was riveted. If my soul had a recording device for capturing moments that alter me, the red Record light would have gone on then. The man next to me whispered, "He was Cassandra. He was a mystic."

On the third floor of the museum, in a circular chamber that felt like the heart of the exhibit, the lyrics of "Imagine," in Lennon's own handwriting, were projected onto the walls. As people circled through the room, sporting Cleveland Indians hats and toting plastic shopping bags, Lennon's words were projected onto their bodies. For a brief moment, the word *peace* alighted on an elderly woman's face. Across the broad shoulders of a man holding his daughter's hand were the words, "I'm a dreamer." I stood still when across my chest ran the line "Live as one."

The second article I carried with me is by the British writer Ian McEwan. I was moved by his emphasis on the power of human love in the wake of the terror on 9/11. He recounted the story of a wife inside one of the hijacked planes, who left a phone message for her sleeping husband in San Francisco:

> There was really only one thing for her to say, those three words that all the terrible art, the worst pop songs and movies, the most seductive lies, can somehow never cheapen. I love you.
>
> She said it over and again before the line went dead. And that is what they were all saying into their phones, from the hijacked planes and the burning towers. There is only love, and then oblivion. Love was all they had to set against the hatred of their murderers.[2]

The word *teleology* comes from the Greek root *telos,* meaning goal or purpose. An action you take or a process you are going through is teleological when it is for the sake of a particular outcome. I kept these two articles with me; they reassured and inspired me because they hinted at a promise that there might be a force within me ceaselessly conspiring to lead me, even when I am not aware of it, to an ultimate goal. They suggested that despite all this fear, within and outside of me, "there is only love."

THE SHEPHERD AND THE NYMPH

There is a statue in the Luxembourg Gardens in Paris that sits at the end of a long, rectangular reflecting pool that has wrought-iron chairs dotting the periphery. The chairs are used by artists and writers and an occasional couple with their seats pulled close for kissing. The first time I approached the statue, I slowed my steps when I saw that it contained not just one form but two. From a distance, the mass of marble looked like the expression of a single, unified gesture. But up close, I could see two gorgeously interwoven bodies. He is semireclining beside her, his upper body propped up on one elbow, as she leans against his raised knee. He is as close to her as he can be. But what I remember about him most vividly is the way his gaze is locked on hers, visibly drinking her in. This look of love breathes life into his chiseled marble face.

She is reclining across his lap, her back arched and her pelvis tilted so that her torso is wide open to him. The intensity of his gaze seems to elicit a reaction from her body as if the love in his eyes could physically touch her.

What breathes life into her is her neck. Her ivory head is tilted back, defenseless. Her exposed neck makes her entire body appear like an offering, a submission. Her posture radiates pure trust. I stood there before them in awe, thinking, *human love can be this holy.* To be this open, this vulnerable, is how the human body transforms into scripture.

Even at those times when the pilgrimage convinced me that, like Teresa of Avila, I could be satisfied now with nothing less than the Divine, I was always fiercely aware of how much I needed a human love, a love to meet me in flesh and blood. Any dualistic ideas that it was spiritual to deny and transcend the body were not true for me.

So why was I on this pilgrimage alone—sans lover, sans even a friend? Was it so unconsciously ingrained that I had to be sexless to approach the Divine? This is when I realized that there was a deeper need for being alone. There was a much harder truth for me to look at, one that the pilgrimage made so apparent that I couldn't ignore it. As a woman, without using my body sexually— without being a girlfriend or potential life partner to some stunning man—I was encountering one of the most intense inner battles I had ever faced: maintaining my own self-worth. Stripped of the usual sources of self-worth for a woman, I found myself on a treacherous see-saw, vacillating between the extremes of feeling free and entirely independent—like Salma Hayek in the movie *Frida,* when she cuts her hair and becomes her own after her husband has betrayed her—to feeling totally alone and ineffectual, my life devoid of purpose and meaning.

I wanted to know my own worth. I wanted to find stable ground within, so that my sense of self-worth was not dependent on anything or anyone external to me. I wanted to find bedrock. I wanted to touch the foundation of my sense of worth, discover what it is built on.

To help with my horrible French accent, I rented every film I could find by the French director Eric Rohmer. It was from watching one of these films that I came across a description of Acis and Galatea, the mythic lovers in the Luxembourg Gardens. In the Rohmer film *Rendezvous in Paris,* a couple is standing beside the statue, while the man explains to the woman who the figures represent. Galatea is a nymph, Acis a shepherd, and they are the embodiment of true love. Hovering over them is the jealous Cyclops Polyphemus, ready to drop a giant boulder on top of the couple at the moment the shepherd embraces the nymph. They have no idea how powerful they have become by exposing themselves to love. Love holds the boulder back, renders the demigod impotent, and immortalizes the lovers' anticipated embrace.

Rilke suggests that if I want a great love in my life, I must act as if I have great work to do. I must go into myself, collect myself, and hold fast to myself. I must be "much alone" and "become something," he maintains. "For believe me, the more one is, the richer is all that one experiences."[3] And only once this becoming more has taken place within will "man and maid" be freed from false identities and be able at last to "seek each other not as opposites but . . . *as human beings.*"[4]

THE LADY AND THE UNICORN

On the second floor of the Musée de Cluny, the National Museum of the Middle Ages in Paris, there is an oval room kept dark, warm, and womblike, where the series of Flemish tapestries known collectively as *The Lady and the Unicorn* are preserved. Five of the tapestries represent the human senses, titled respectively *Taste, Touch, Smell, Hearing,* and *Sight.* The sixth and last represents a sense that is not quite as straightforward as the rest, or at least not quite as well developed. The banner that waves above the Lady in the last tapestry reads À Mon Seul Désir. Translation: To My Own (or Only) Desire.

Some believe that the message À Mon Seul Désir suggests that the maiden is taking off her jewels to renounce the world of material reality so that she can enter the world of spirit. This would then mean that the sixth sense, the final tapestry of *The Lady and the Unicorn,* is a visual representation of the idea that the body and the material world must be transcended before the soul can be wedded to the Divine.

However, the popular vote in 15th-century France was for the interpretive slant that the sixth sense was that of the heart. Imagine it: the heart as a sense as developed and utilized as our capacity to taste or touch. The heart was understood to be not just an organ but a spiritual chamber, a meeting place, a field of inner divinity. The heart was where the human and the Divine comingled, where one was within the other in a state of union.

Under the banner with the motto To My Own Desire is the entrance to the pavilion, or tentlike structure in the center of the tapestry. The flaps are parted slightly in a way that lets the viewer (or me, at least) imagine that after taking off her jewels, the lady will then step out of her royal clothes and enter the tent, leaving the external world as naked and revealed as she came into it.

But what does all this suggest?

In a pamphlet I found at the museum's gift shop, I read a passage that sounded like one of the missing keys to the mystery of the final tapestry: "In chevaleresque literature the pavilion often represented the symbolic mediator between the profane and the sacred, the human and the divine." In the tapestry, the unicorn is holding a heraldic flag with three crescent moons running diagonally across it. The crescent moon is one of the oldest known symbols, with a variety of meanings. Here it could suggest the rise of the Divine Feminine that occurred during the Middles Ages.

As I stood before the tapestry, I was as transfixed by this unicorn as I was by the one I saw in the Met as a teenager. I stared at it, trying to figure out what it could possibly represent. What did the unicorn have to do with my sense of self-worth and my relationship to my body?

Rilke, in *The Sonnets to Orpheus,* describes the unicorn as "the creature that never was." Rilke speculates that the people who beheld this creature fed it "not with any grain, but always with just the thought that it might be." And then with its one white horn, the unicorn "approached a virgin to be inside the mirror and in her."[5]

The correlation between the maid, or the virgin, and the unicorn is uncovered in *The Physiologus*, a bestiary of compiled myths of various species written in the 3rd century in Alexandria. It relates that only the virgin can tame the wild, sacred creature. And the gesture of this "taming" is the moment when the unicorn places its horn in her lap.[6]

I lost my virginity, if virginity can be lost, to a woman. I know this might not make sense, but let me explain.

The first time I had sex with a man I was numb to the experience. There wasn't pain, but there also wasn't any pleasure. He was too young and maybe too inexperienced to notice that I was never really there with him. I had an inability to be present, to be in my body when we were intimate.

I don't know if I ever loved him. I never considered my own feelings. I only knew that he desired me. I then felt obligated to please him. I never asked myself whether I wanted him, whether I was in love with him. I remember him asking me one night if I regretted losing my virginity. His tone infuriated me. It seemed as if he was letting me know that he had taken something from me only now that I could never get it back. I was so confused. How could I have lost something when I never felt anything? And why was he exempt from that subtraction of worth? Why did a negation of worth only apply to me?

When he broke up with me for God, considering me the "forbidden fruit," and moved to Israel to join a Hasidic community, I turned vegan, went to Smith College, and took a hiatus from men.

I was with a woman mainly because I could be intimate with her without needing to vacate my skin. I felt safe to be fully in my body, to feel how fathomless I am. And I felt *more* because of her, never *less*. I never even entertained the idea of my worth depreciating because of our pleasure. She helped reveal to me my own depths. She helped me remember what it felt like to be my own again. To be one-in-myself.

One of the definitions of virgin is "without alloy or admixture," as in virgin gold. It refers to a substance that is made up of just one element. Describing a person, virgin is most often understood to mean a woman who has never had intercourse. But I felt that the virgin who could tame the unicorn represented a oneness, a unity that nothing external to her could take away. Rather than having anything to do with sex or gender, virginity depends on something far more integral to our being and yet far less apparent—something that each of us can only perceive and claim within.

Aside from my obsession with the infinity symbol, math has never made any sense to me, especially when it comes to the addition and subtraction of a woman's worth based on her sexual experience. In terms of women's sexual history, I realize that in the pre–paternity test era a woman who could unequivocally carry on a family's bloodline was worth her weight in gold. But today the shadow of that outdated virgin currency still lingers, in destructive self-worth issues for women who feel like they are less or deserve less because they have had many sexual partners, in women who have never really experienced the depth of their own body's pleasure in order to remain more "virginal," in the catastrophic reality of young girls in the sex slave industry being sold to the highest bidder.

The Lady, the Maiden, and the Virgin are archetypes long overdue for reinvention. My vote is that from here on, virginity should be considered the ultimate "I Am," or the proverbial "Yes" that comes from claiming and defining oneself from within. Virginity applies to both sexes equally, not just women. It's the word that signifies self-possession. To be virginal is to recognize oneself as one inviolable whole.

Marion Woodman might interpret my interest in the unicorn as an unconscious knowing that "the unicorn symbolizes the creative power of the spirit and was seen in medieval times as an allegory of Christ."[7] At the time of the pilgrimage I was certainly asleep to any Christlike correlations in my attraction to the unicorn, but I did sense the unicorn's power. For me, the unicorn began to represent a possible state of being—a pure, innocent, and Divine Love. And as I stared at the sixth tapestry in the Musée de Cluny, I knew that the Lady became the Virgin again, or for the first time, only once she entered the tent, the place of the heart. This is where the unicorn, or Divine Love, can lay its horn in her lap.

Margaret Starbird, a writer and researcher of the Divine Feminine, interprets the sixth tapestry of *The Lady and the Unicorn* through the love poetry found in the Old Testament, in the Song of Songs. According to Starbird, the banner above the Lady relates to the passage "His banner over me is love."[8] The tent, she says, represents the sanctuary in the Song of Songs: "The tent is the bridal chamber of the Sacred Marriage, where the Bride awaits her Bridegroom: 'Let my lover come into his garden and taste its choice fruits.'"[9]

According to Starbird's research, the letter *A* in the tapestry's banner is, "a stylized glyph for *aleph* and *tau*, the alpha and omega of the Hebrew alphabet,"[10] which translate as the First and the Last. The symbolism of the Alpha and the Omega and the reoccurring presence of the letter *X* in the tapestries represent the union of male and female in holy partnership. The ancient and archetypal *V*, the feminine chalice, and *^*, the masculine blade, are symbols for male and female, Starbird suggests, depicting "an ancient dualism that can be reconciled to the age-old paradigm of wholeness."[11] The male has to become female, and the female male; the opposites, as in the First and the Last, have to be made one.

This reconciliation has to take place for wholeness—for virginity, integrity—to be remembered. Knowing our worth has everything to do with bringing together within us what we have thought were opposites: Divine and human, male and female, masculine and feminine, light and dark, virgin and whore.

I had never read the Song of Songs before the pilgrimage. But from my research I knew that in the Middle Ages there was a curious correlation between the experience of the senses, especially the sixth sense of the heart, and the Song of Songs.

It was during the Middle Ages when the tapestries were created that the Song of Songs reached the peak of its readership and commentary. It was accorded more commentaries than any other book in the Old Testament—30 in the 12th century alone.[12]

One of the most prolific commentators, Bernard of Clairvaux, referred to the Song as "the book of experience."[13] For him, the experience was of love itself:

> Love is alone sufficient by itself; it pleases by itself, and for its own sake. It is itself a merit, and itself its own recompense. It seeks neither cause, nor consequences, beyond itself. It is its own fruit, its own object and usefulness. I love, because I love; I love, that I may love.[14]

The Cluny tapestries, especially the sixth, could suggest that it is only through the human senses that the Divine aperture of the heart is opened. The act of the Lady turning to go within the tent could be understood as the moment of embodiment when she at last receives herself—all of herself, not just the good and the light and the easy to see but also the painful and discarded parts of herself.

It is this pure feminine energy, according to Woodman, that allows a woman to quietly, triumphantly, turn within and love even what had before been deemed unworthy of love. Both "unpossessed and unpossessing," this energy exudes, paradoxically, that "its strength is its vulnerability."[15] However, "until a woman can receive herself," Woodman warns, "she will unconsciously force others to reject her, despite the fact that her most conscious desire is to be loved."[16]

This unreceived woman? I was she.

Love for my soul came effortlessly. What I had to find, what I had to come to love, was my own vulnerability—the places that are darkest and most human in me. I had to find a way to redeem what I still felt was unworthy, the part of me that my love had yet to reach.

The Red Virgin

When the Christian mystic Simone Weil had her first encounter with the Divine, it came in what she described as "a moment of intense physical suffering."[17] She had been forcing herself to feel love; she made the act of loving a spiritual practice, a sort of sacred form of "fake it till you make it." She had memorized the poem "Love" by George Herbert, and was repeating it as if it were a mantra. The recitation of this poem incited an experience of the Divine that Weil would later remember as "a presence more personal, more certain, more real than that of a human being."[18] The last lines of the poem read: "You must sit down, sayes Love, and taste my meat: / So I did sit and eat."[19]

In his introduction to *Waiting for God*, a collection of Weil's letters and essays, Leslie Fiedler notes that food played a dominant role in Weil's life "from her childhood refusal of sugar through her insistence at Le Puy on eating only as much as the relief allowance of the unemployed, to her death from semistarvation in England."[20]

I followed in Weil's imagined footsteps down to Le Puy, a small provincial town in South Central France where she taught briefly. Earlier dubbed "the Red Virgin" for her uncompromising radical politics, Weil is said to have "horrified the good citizens of Le Puy"[21] with her support for the working classes, including picketing with the unemployed and joining them in their "pick and shovel work."[22]

For most of her short life, Weil felt spiritually compelled to remain outside of any religious tradition. She was magnetized by a passion and fascination with the Catholic Church, and yet she resisted baptism. As I read her theology, I kept feeling like I could see through her. It seemed to me that she spent so much of her life struggling with not feeling good enough, not feeling worthy. Our similarities were not lost on me.

Weil started her "Cahiers," or notebooks, in the town of Le Puy. We both began charting the interior as teenagers. And I went to Le Puy at about the same age as Weil: we were both in our mid-20s and both rail thin. I wasn't rationing my food, though. I ate duck practically every day, mainly because *confit de canard* was the easiest thing on the menu to say. And I ate French fries like it was a requirement for being in France. Yet as the weeks passed, it was undeniably clear that I was losing weight.

I know this might sound strange, but my body shrinks when I don't have a lover. It's as if through touch it receives something vital—an intangible nourishment—that food alone doesn't supply. Regardless of my caloric intake, without the physical love and presence of another, my body goes through an adult version of "failure to thrive." So I arrived in Le Puy much as Weil arrived: young, too thin, theologically versed, and in exile from the kind of spiritual home the church can provide.

When I first learned about Weil's untimely death in her early 30s, I had an Achilles–Patroclus moment. In *The Iliad*, Achilles and Patroclus are war buddies, perhaps war buddies with benefits, and their love and understanding of each other is epic. Patroclus steals Achilles's armor and faces a deadly foe in the hopes of sparing his friend's life. Achilles watches as Patroclus dies in the effort to save him, and because Patroclus is wearing his armor, Achilles has a moment of coming face-to-face with his own mortality. Patroclus's self-sacrifice marks a turning point in *The Iliad*, when Achilles is motivated by love to not only return to battle but also return more fully to life.

I arrived in Le Puy late at night and picked an inn solely because its sign was in neon red. The raucous sound of birds outside my bedroom woke me too early the next morning. I tried to go back to sleep but couldn't; my eyes kept fluttering open in anticipation. I walked to the window and slowly opened the vertical panels of the wooden shutters covering each window. As the cool air hit my warm skin, I realized my body felt fragile and achy.

At breakfast I asked the innkeepers how to reach the cathedral. They both smiled and said, "Go up." I smiled back but wasn't sure if they were attempting metaphysics over eggs or were giving me literal directions. I resolved to ask someone on my way. I left my suitcase at the inn and took to the streets.

The first person I came across was an elderly lady with a baguette peeking out of her cloth grocery bag. Her upper body was curved so far forward that she was looking down at her feet. She raised her head as I asked directions, then waved her arm in the air. "Up there" was all she said.

I realized then that the cathedral must be at the top of the hill that the town of Le Puy surrounds. I began to climb upward, still wishing I had a street name to look for or a sense of where exactly "up there" was located. I wound up and up, picking streets by chance, until the medieval cathedral of Le Puy came spiraling into view.

Le Puy Cathedral, or Notre-Dame du Puy-en-Velay, contains two Black Madonnas—one in the winter chapel that was most likely brought from Egypt during the Crusades and another in the main sanctuary that has more European features. I entered the cathedral slowly, with furtive glances to the left and right to see if anyone else was there. I didn't want to be observed. Once inside, I headed straight for the winter chapel. The small sanctuary was empty. I found myself blissfully alone under the fiery gaze of this dark-skinned Madonna.

I recalled with awe that she had once been blamed for a plague that had swept the town and had been burned for it. But paradoxically, she has also been venerated for centuries as Le Puy's fertility goddess. For hundreds of years, innumerable women have approached her out of a desperate desire for a child. Some are driven by a need from within, others by a need to maintain their social standing and fulfill their obligations as wives. I could feel the presence of all those women. Their ardent belief in the Black Madonna hung thick in the air around her, as if past miracles had left palpable remains.

I slowed as I approached her. Icons of saints were painted on the stone wall of the small sanctum. I acknowledged them with a slight nod as if they were the Madonna's keepers and then continued with unhurried steps toward her. The aisle led right to her feet. It was only when I got close that I noticed the child on her lap. Both Madonna and child were dressed in the same type of garb, although the stripes and colors differed.

I sat down in the first pew as something clamored to come to consciousness. I needed to be still, very quiet. It was then that I noticed I was burning with fever. I thought of a line by William Blake, the 18th-century poet and mystic: "The voice of honest indignation is the voice of God." Honest indignation: that is what I felt. With the Black Madonna's image before me, I thought of the separation of sexuality and spirituality in most religions. Acutely aware of my feverish, overheated body, I recognized that I couldn't have a spiritual experience without the body. The physical is spiritual, and the spiritual is physical: there is no separation, in my experience. How had the body, especially the female body, been divested of its Divine worth?

Even today, the church assigns sexuality to the female body.[23] The body is *materia*, human, woman, blood, and procreation—all secondary to the higher attributes of soul or spirit, mind, and the Divine, which are ascribed to the male.[24] And this has always been so—the reason why, from the Talmud to the New Testament to the Koran, women have been asked to remain silent, why their experience is not considered of equal value to that of men.

I looked down at my hands, resting in my lap, palms up. I wasn't aware I had placed them there. What happened next can no doubt be attributed at least in part to the fact that I had a raging fever. But I couldn't stop staring at my hands. They weren't glowing or displaying the stigmata, but I was fixated on them, acutely aware that they were *mine*. I had never before acknowledged the presence, the *reality* of my body. What struck me in that moment was that for my entire life I had taken my body for granted. I had never hated my body, but I also had never felt grateful for it. It had been overlooked and undervalued.

In that moment I was flooded with emotion and curled forward over my hands. I remembered that the flesh is innocent. My flesh is pure, loyal, devoted. My body is wedded to my soul. Being human is the other half of a Divine equation, not separate from it. The Divine couldn't be here without the body. I was looking at my hands the way the Shepherd looks at the Nymph in that statue in the Luxembourg Gardens.

I had never felt so loved, so wholly my own.

Something surfaced from deep in my unconscious— what Carl Jung would deem the *de profundis levantus*— and with it the fever took hold of me. My eyes seared with hot tears that spilled onto the floor near my feet.

The flesh is innocent, I repeated to myself. *The body is intrinsically good.*

I can't really explain what happened next. I guess it's something that passes in the deepest places and can never really be described. In those silent moments when I was curled forward over my hands before the Black Madonna in Le Puy's winter chapel, I sensed a consciousness as fierce and clear as light, as pure and holy as the Divine, in the least expected place, the flesh.

And then I found myself hurrying toward the first and only nun I saw, who happened to be working the register at the cathedral gift shop. In unbroken French that I was only able to muster in that moment of necessity, I related a vision of light within the body, of the Divine experienced and perceived through the spiritual sense of the heart. She could tell I had been crying. And when she looked me in the eyes, I knew immediately that I could have said far less and she would have heard me. She knew exactly what I meant.

The kindness and level of recognition in the soft eyes of Sister Odile calmed me. She gently placed her hand on my shoulder and told me that I was not alone in this understanding, that many have experienced the wisdom of the Black Madonna as the light, as the fires of love that can only be found within this very human body.

Then Sister Odile asked me if I knew why the Black Madonna was black. Before I could respond, she continued on with a historical account of the Madonna in the winter chapel. I already knew that the icon's dark skin represents her Egyptian ethnicity, but Sister Odile also offered a mystical explanation: the Black Madonna is dark because she burned from the inside out, turning the color that represents union with the Divine. "Black," the nun said, "is the color that has absorbed all other colors. The Black Madonna is black from the love she has found within her, a love that burns eternally in the heart."

As I was leaving the gift shop, Sister Odile called out to me, and looking me seriously in the eyes asked, "Have you read the Song of Songs?" When I shook my head no, she said sternly yet lovingly, "Read it now!"

Visionary artist and musician Lynda McClanahan articulates the powerful effect the Song can have on its readers:

> It has the same power to dissolve the brain into the heart as a Zen koan and deftly wears down nearly every boundary we can think of. Because the poem has this effect, it blurs the edges between the lovers, between God and the individual soul, between Yahweh and Israel, and even between culture and whatever it is we would be without it.[25]

The Song suggests that life is the paradoxical comingling of both the Divine and the human. This paradigm of a both/and rather than either/or allows the sacred and the profane, the Divine and the human to coexist, to be held in such a way that the lover in the Song of Songs can be both penetrating the woman from within her, as an inner light in a state of spiritual union, and also from outside her, in physical lovemaking. The back and forth of the lover and beloved in the Song, the tease of finding each other only to part again, is the sacred dance of becoming more naked, more fully revealed to the Divine.

Jungian analyst Marie-Louise von Franz holds that the mysterious alchemical text *Aurora Consurgens* most likely has its origin in Saint Thomas Aquinas's interpretation of the Song.[26] It concerns the process of death, the end of which is "the mystical marriage, or love experience . . . with the other half of the personality."[27] Legend has it that in the midst of Aquinas's last sermon on the Song, he died just as he interpreted the words, "Come, my beloved, let us go into the field."[28]

Aurora Consurgens forewarns any pilgrim that the path to find "the Wisdom of God" is grueling and deathly long, and yet "to find her only one thing is needed."[29] The text assures us that once Wisdom is found, "she is a kind of eternal nourishment, or something like a fire which can light other fires."[30]

I felt very in touch with this fire as I reentered the main sanctuary of the cathedral. I was sweating from the heat. This is when I first noticed the fever stone in a recessed alcove to the left of the main altar of the Black Madonna. The legend of the stone dates back to the 1st century. Supposedly, a woman with a deathly fever fell asleep on the stone, and when she awoke, her fever was miraculously gone. While lying on the stone, the woman had a vision of the Virgin Mary, who told her to build a cathedral there. The earliest pilgrims to Le Puy's fever stone included the Emperor Charlemagne in the 8th century and two centuries later, Pope Leo IX, who declared Le Puy the most important shrine to Mary in France.

A blue velvet rope hung between me and the fever stone, preventing me from touching it. As I headed toward the alcove, I noticed a notebook resting on the edge of the Black Madonna's shrine. Turning to the first blank page, I took out a red pen and started writing, so passionately that my pen tore through the paper. I was writing out vows to my own soul. And I signed my vows with a new name, a resurrected moniker: the Red Virgin.

Then I crossed the line, going where I clearly had no right to go. I leapt over the velvet rope like an Olympic hurdler and walked up to the fever stone as if the Madonna herself had decreed that this lonely little fevered foreigner was worthy of such proximity.

And so I did what I felt I had to do: I pressed my body, pulsing with heat and tangled emotions, against the fever stone. Spreading my arms out wide on either side of me and stretching my legs out straight, I made a cross of my body. Now imagine you were above me just in that moment I decided to press my skin to the fever stone. You can see me turn my head from left to right, as I pressed each cheek firmly against the cool surface of the stone. Then watch as I leaned forward and pressed my lips against two narrow ridges on the stone's surface for an unrushed kiss.

What you cannot see is my smile when my own warmth, from my nearness to the stone, came back to caress my face. The smile came from remembering that Simone Weil's experience of Divine Love was right here, as it is for me, "at the intersection of body and soul."[31]

THE ANGEL AND THE ANTHROPOS

The second time I saw Saint Sarah-La-Kali, the day was uncommonly bright. From my hotel room I looked up and saw an impossibly cerulean-blue sky. Arles, known for the fields of sunflowers that are so gorgeously captured by Van Gogh, was the closest city to Saintes-Maries-de-la-Mer I could travel to by train. I got dressed and buzzed around my room with the kind of amped up energy I usually get from overdosing on dark chocolate. Clearly, I was excited to see Saint Sarah again.

Jean-Pierre, my cab driver, was waiting outside my hotel. He had the windows of his taxi rolled down, and the radio was blasting hypnotic music. It reminded me of being swept inside the crypt with the procession on my first pilgrimage. The Romani language itself was music to my ears, as if a long-forgotten cadence that articulated a colorful and rootless side of myself I could forget but never lose.

The taxi sped along the road that snakes through the Carmargue to Saintes-Maries-de-la-Mer as if it had every turn memorized; Jean-Pierre was barely touching the wheel. He seemed to be off in a reverie as the car whisked us past pink flamingos and heron, drawing nearer and nearer to the sea.

Jean-Yves Leloup, in his translation from the Coptic of *The Gospel of Mary Magdalene*, relates Mary's emphasis on the "true human being" to Gita Mallasz's transcription of *Talking with Angels*. Both texts, according to Leloup, bring forth "the possibility of the birth in us of the authentic human, which is none other than the theandros, [or the Anthropos] the divine-human."[32]

On Friday, October 29, 1943, as the Nazi regime reached deeper into the hills of Budapest, Gita Mallasz and her friends heard a voice that said, "You yourself are the bridge."[33] It was eventually revealed that the wise, clear voice each of them heard was the voice of their corresponding angel. According to the seven angels, the true human is someone capable of being a bridge between the material world and the ethereal realms, one who has reconciled the opposites from within. The angels restored a sense of dignity and worth to being human by explaining that we all contain this potential to be a part of both the created and the creating world— both fully embodied and directly connected to spirit. The true human can remember the Divine within and use that consciousness to help create reality through the infinite grace and power of the "I Am."

Leloup interprets Jesus's teachings in the Gospel of Mary as a "ceaseless recollection" in order to hem together the memory of the full human—of the capacity of the human that is one with the Divine within.[34] He conjectures that the Magdalene, having "recollected" or integrated the memory of her full humanity, which includes her divinity, had a kind of clairvoyance, or clear seeing, that permitted her to live out her last 30 years in the dark caverns and caves east of Marseilles, in the South of France.[35]

In the 4th century, Christianity's first ecumenical council, held at Nicaea, declared that Jesus was *homoousios*—of the same substance as the Divine and yet also fully human. By the mid 5th century, the hypostatic union, the unity of Christ's divinity and humanity, was a part of the creed of Orthodox Christianity. This theological fact drop-kicked me when I first came across it in seminary. It suggests that the human and the Divine are not above and below one another but rather at the same level or, if you will, intersecting. The transcendent and the immanent are face-to-face. Or I can explain it this way. Imagine the Divine is a large circle. Then draw yourself as a circle inside that circle. You and your humanity are not above or below the Divine; you are concentric to what is most sacred.

Jean-Pierre dropped me off at Saint Sarah-La-Kali's crypt, the Queen of the Outsiders, and went to meet a friend at a nearby bar. I entered the crypt alone. Unlike the first time I approached this small and powerful icon, there were no eyes on me as I drew near.

Hundreds of small votives burned on either side of Saint Sarah, their flames flicking like tiny tongues as I walked by. The air was thick with silence. I embraced Saint Sarah the way the woman with the mapped face had taught me years earlier. I brought my face close to hers and rubbed each of my cheeks against hers and then slid my thumb down the bridge of her nose. Our reunion complete, I let the silence and her presence overcome me.

I imagined what it must have felt like for Mary Magdalene, if the legend was true, to be here in the south of France with her daughter, an outcast—her spiritual authority never validated.

The scholar Jane Schaberg, author of *The Resurrection of Mary Magdalene,* had an ardent wish of hearing these words from Mary Magdalene's gospel ring out for everyone to hear: "If the Savior considered her to be worthy, who are you to disregard her?"[36]

Yes. Who was I to disregard the Magdalene's spiritual authority? And who was I to disregard my own?

Worth is not given, it's claimed. According to early Christian texts like *The Gospel of Mary Magdalene* and the *Pistis Sophia,* Mary Magdalene was connected to Jesus through visions she experienced in her heart, both during his life and after his resurrection. She had a direct connection to the Divine from within, regardless of whether or not that connection was ever validated externally. Her authority came from her experience.

The original definition of *theologian* didn't refer to someone who systematically and rationally studies religion, as it does today. Before the 9th century, a theologian was someone who had direct experience of the Divine. The word itself derives from the Greek *theos* (θεός), meaning God, and *logia* (λόγια), meaning utterances, sayings, or discourses. A theologian had an intimate, personal experience of the Divine, an inner dialogue, a relationship. It was from this immediate encounter that a theologian spoke with authority.

I was alone in Saint Sarah's crypt, but I still found it difficult to say out loud what I needed to. Now I knew what I had come back to do—to give myself what I had been hoping to get out of degrees from Ivy League schools. I had come to validate the truth of my spiritual experience. The words, when I finally said them, echoed. I didn't speak loudly or forcefully. My voice was low but strong. Each word fell heavily, like a stone I had been carrying around for far too long:

I.

Am.

Worthy.

THE LINEAGE

We are worthy of love just as we are. And we are worthy of what our heart desires.

The volcanic rock our worth rests on is the truth that we don't earn love. A veil lifts with the understanding that we are worthy of love simply because we exist. This is what we have to recognize: our Divine worth as women, not for what we can do or say or provide or heal, but just for the truth of it. Then the choice to get married or be partnered, to have or not have children, to devote our lives to work or service doesn't come from a sense of seeking to fulfill our own self-worth. Our worth is already realized, recognized, revealed. We can make choices for our lives from a place of conscious clarity, rather than out of an unconscious compulsion.

We can heal the past right now in this moment. All we need to do is give ourselves the love we didn't know how to give ourselves before. Maybe you've never allowed yourself to be with the partner you long for most. Maybe you've never been in your body fully enough to feel pleasure. Maybe you haven't yet felt the inherent worth of your body. Maybe you haven't let your love extend to the place where your life has seemed darkest, where your deepest regrets live. Maybe you still hold the idea that your worth is determined by something or someone outside of you. And yet the Divine is not out there, somewhere entirely beyond us. In being human, we are both mortal and immortal.

Symeon the New Theologian was one of the last saints in the Eastern Orthodox Church to argue for the original definition of a theologian as someone who has direct experience of the Divine. He wrote about the succession of spiritual authority, passed down through the church fathers from one generation to the next. But he also spoke of a golden chain, an unbroken lineage of spiritual transmission that wasn't passed visibly through the church but invisibly through charisma—through the humility and audacity of those who connected to the Divine within.

I like to imagine that this unbroken golden chain exists as an unseen but no less real lineage of women who have come to understand that we aver our own spiritual authority through experience, through knowing. We acknowledge our inherent worth and the voice of Divine

Love inside us. It starts with a look of unfaltering love. It starts by allowing our love to reach where it never has before—to our humanity, to the broken places within.

We stand up for who we are. And we give up trying to prove our worth. That's a burden we were never meant to carry. We don't become worthy of love at some point; love is a gift that comes with being. We recognize that it was always ours to claim.

The Fifth Veil

REVEAL Your Inner Mystic

*Say alchemy to most people and they will say,
"Turn metal into gold." Yet what Paracelsus and
the alchemists wanted was to make themselves the
living gold. The treasure without moth or rust, spirit
(pneuma) unalloyed.*

—JEANETTE WINTERSON

THE SPIRITUAL CLOSET

I think we are all hiding. And not without good reason. We have a collective memory of being burned at the stake. Our crime? We revealed that the source of our true power is in our connection to the Divine, which is within. And if we are directly connected to the Divine within, then no institution or individual can mediate or regulate this, and no one can profit from the illusion that only the ordained are holy enough for proximity to the sacred.

Fortunately, setting a woman, a mystic, a heretic, a witch on fire in public is no longer socially acceptable. And calling someone a *witch* is inching its way back to the compliment it always should have been.

So why are we still hiding?

This is what I believe: we are all far stranger than we allow ourselves to see.

I've always loved the card game Bullshit, mostly because it's so refreshing and cathartic to say what I know and to call out someone when I know they're bluffing about the cards they've been dealt. At some indiscernible point, I started an internal game of Bullshit. The cards were events, experiences, happenings in my life that I tried at times to gloss over, to make seem normal, to explain away.

There is something incendiary about telling the truth about our real experiences with the Divine. As if we might still get burned for displaying the power we each contain.

Jeffrey Kripal, in his study of mysticism, suggests that we have grown too complacent with the expectation of normalcy:

> There is a Presence rooted in our erotic forms, which we boringly call bodies, and in our nocturnal visions, which we banally call dreams, within which, out of which we think and write. We have become too familiar with ourselves and our strange existences; it is time to become strange again.[1]

Call it what you want—the Superman Complex, the Peter Parker syndrome—hiding a huge aspect of who we are, of being one thing yet pretending to be another, is a divided life. Keeping our divinity in the dark is taxing. I think we're done. It's too much of a hassle.

We have worn out the fertility of this viewpoint, and it's time to stop investing in the limits we've identified with and start believing in the impossible, the ineffable, that lives in and through us all the time. It's time to come out of the spiritual closet. We need to let our own mystery breathe. It's time to unlock the chains we have placed on the most magical aspect of our being and let our inner mystic go for a walk around the neighborhood in broad daylight.

If you tell me that your life is boring, that nothing extraordinary has ever happened; if you have been waiting for someone else to know that you are so much more than the normal façade you present to others; if you have been seeking validation of your "weirdness" outside of yourself, consider this sentence my silent nod. I see you. I am calling your bluff.

Lay your cards on the table.

I know you're human. But I also know you're Divine.

DR. UNNO AND THE DISAPPEARING ACT

I started meditating out of necessity. My nervous system had me at gunpoint. I had to dispel the waves of anxiety that racked my mind and body at the oddest moments. Several months after Flight U.S. Scare, I was diagnosed with GAD (Generalized Anxiety Disorder). My whole body screamed "lions and tigers and bears" while I was sitting quietly reading a book in the library, trying to act like a normal college student. My eyes would dart for the Exit sign; my heart would lodge in my throat, banging against my vocal cords prepared to cry for help; and my legs would jolt with rivulets of energy, ready to run like Speedy Gonzales to save my own sweet hide.

The contradiction was nearly humorous. Nearly. The not-so-funny part about GAD was that it began to tether me to my dorm room so I could avoid getting caught in public when a panic attack hit. I was offered antianxiety medications, which at times were helpful, necessary. But I knew my body was telling me something. There was a part of me that didn't want to cover up the anxiety or numb it out. I wanted to go into it. I knew that if I didn't face the anxiety, it could derail my entire life. Meditation was not just to help me stay calm: it was truly about finding a way to save my life from the inside out.

Taitetsu Unno, a Smith College professor and Shin Buddhist minister, taught insight meditation in the basement of a church on campus. I attended each session with the ardor and conviction of a new AA member. I appeared normal, I'm sure, but most of the time, I was ready to bolt through the nearest window. I was riddled with anxiety that felt like electrified barbed wire coursing through my veins the moment I tried to sit still and slow down the internal chatter.

Dr. Unno was my Mr. Miyagi, the fictional karate master in *The Karate Kid* films. He only spoke in simple, complete, declarative sentences. In all my years of knowing him, he never uttered a run-on sentence. He was the epitome of tranquility. I wanted what he had. I wanted to know how to have such profound inner peace.

I remember running to Dr. Unno's office when I saw that he had received the best student reviews of the entire Smith faculty. I was so proud. I read him some of the raves the students had written about his courses and meditation instruction. His inner pool remained placid. Nothing I said affected him for better or worse.

He said that if he were happy about the positive comments, he would be unhappy about the comments that expressed the opposite. This incessant calm was what I encountered no matter what I brought to Dr. Unno. I could tell him the most whacky and bizarre visions I had while meditating, and he heard each story with the same unflagging peace. I couldn't impress or disturb him.

But then I disappeared. This, I felt certain, would at least raise an eyebrow. Here's what I told him: I had lit a candle beside my icon of Kali, which I did each time before I started to meditate. I was watching the undulating rhythm of the flame, the way it looked like the movement a tongue would make to form speech. Kali's mantra was playing itself in the back of my thoughts as if it were a recording on auto-replay. Rather than focusing on objects in the external world, I redirected my sight inward.

What emotions, what feelings were living in me, informing my thoughts and subsequently my actions? I sensed tension in my gut, fear in my chest, and a thought ricocheting throughout my body that chanted, "You are a panic attack! You are a panic attack! You are a panic attack."

I released the tension and fear through breathwork. Then I chased down that renegade chant and edited it so that it said, "I am free. I am free. I am free," announcing it through an inner loudspeaker to all areas of my body.

Then there was nothing. Literally. I sensed an emptiness. I opened my eyes, and all the objects around me were divested of their usual meaning. They didn't have a name or a place. My body moved with unusual fluidity to stand in front of the mirror. I was weightless, transparent, as empty as the objects around me. My reflection seemed as insubstantial as a hologram.

Every story I once held about myself had vacated me, every last word. "I" was nowhere to be found. I realized that my idea of who I am is as much a construct as all the beautiful possessions and things around me. This was terrifying. But it was also the truest taste of reality I had ever known. If my understanding of myself was constructed, then it also meant it could be deconstructed, rewritten, made entirely new.

When I recounted this experience to Dr. Unno, he was as unimpressed as ever, maybe even borderline bored. Then he said something thoroughly unexpected that made my disappearing act go *poof.*

"It is not necessary to talk about revelation. Be it."

THE POSSUM

As life coach Martha Beck was writing *Finding Your Way in a Wild New World,* about making things happen with ease, she kept encountering the kinds of people her book was about: shamans, healers, and mystics from traditions all over the world. She thought that when she finished writing, the encounters would stop. But they didn't.

Shortly after completing the book, Martha was introduced to a shaman from South America and invited to attend a retreat he was leading. Martha has been leading retreats for years, but she had never attended one led by someone else. Her anxiety went for broke.

The only thing that calms her down without fail is an animal, any animal. Even, she explains, "If I woke up and there was a rat in my room, I would be profoundly calm." So as she was heading to the retreat, Martha decided to request that an animal be sent to her, to relieve her anxiety about meeting the shaman. She sat in her car and mentally called for a pronghorn antelope to cross her path. Four hours later, as she was making her way toward the retreat center, she saw a blur of sand-colored objects moving quickly before her. She stopped her car when she realized that she was staring right at a herd of pronghorn antelope.

Martha sat in her car laughing and gasping, flooded with awe. Any lingering disbelief she may have had about the bond that exists between animals and humans dissolved. Shamans are known for their ability to communicate with the spirit world, including the spirits of animals. Before Martha had even begun the retreat, she had experienced that there is something real in the practices of those who have found a way to connect with the natural world. She had concrete evidence that magic is real.

One of the most important things I learned at Harvard Divinity School was to become conscious of that kind of power—the kind of calling out from within that allowed Martha Beck to conjure her pronghorns. The capacity for it has always been there, I believe, since I was a little girl. But it took a possum on my fire escape for me to finally take it seriously.

At the time, I was studying mystics throughout history, specifically female mystics and saints in various traditions. Surrender was up for me big-time. I knew it was what I most needed to do, and it was the single most frequently used word among the female mystics I was reading about. But as a fiery, independent young woman I was allergic to the word *surrender*. I had no idea how to swallow it, much less work it into my life.

Enter the possum.

At about three o'clock one morning, a possum waddled off the limb of a nearby tree and climbed halfway down the fire escape outside my bedroom window. The weight of him rattling around woke me. When I looked out the window into his beady little M&M eyes, right at the level of mine, I freaked out and huddled immobilized beneath my covers.

From the moment I saw the possum I knew why he was there and what his presence meant. But I pretended I didn't. I wouldn't let myself believe that life could be that magical. I wasn't ready to accept that the universe, or the Divine, or whatever is binding us all together in unseen ways, cared enough about me in particular to show me what my soul needed to learn.

Every once in a while, I would pull out my deck of Karen Vogel and Vicki Nobel's MotherPeace tarot cards and spread them out in a fan before me. I never learned the "official" way to read them. I would just pick the card that my soul-voice led me to choose in response to the question, "What do I need to know most in this moment?"

For days before the possum arrived, I kept pulling the Surrender card. And yes, the Surrender card has a picture of a person hanging upside down in a tree, possum-style, symbolizing surrender to shamanic death and rebirth, or to unconditional love. I had set the card on my altar as my wish.

The first night the possum arrived, I called it a fluke. I shook it off and went about my life the next day actively denying that his visit held any meaning or had any connection to the Tarot card on my altar. I went so far as to call myself loopy, strange, and solipsistic for considering, even momentarily, that some part of me might be able to communicate with animals.

You know that moment in horror movies, when the killer is finally slain and there's a split second of calm, and then just as we start to relax, the killer comes back for that last stab at our hero, and we scream from the soles of our feet? Well, that's how I greeted the possum on the night of his second visit. I peeled paint from the walls with my screaming. And just as in the horror movies we know deep down that the killer's not really dead, and we're expecting that final appearance, I screamed because some part of me had known all along that the possum would return.

And in returning, he validated that knowing. The same unnameable part of me that knew why he had come in the first place was the same part of me that knew he would return.

The experience of surrender is not synonymous with submission, as I had anticipated it would be. Surrendering is more akin to committing to something with spiritual blood, sweat, and tears. Surrender is an inner act. It has nothing to do with anything or anyone external to us, though it can affect every one of our interactions and relationships.

Surrendering is a soul capacity that must be flexed and developed like any bicep or tricep. It allows us to move deeper, move further into who we truly are. Surrender aligns us only with what's true for us. It disengages us from the surface drama of life, as entertaining as that may be, and takes us beneath the waves of who we try to be and who we want to be, letting us rest in who we truly are.

I knew the possum had come to turn my life upside down or, rather, inside out. His arrival showed me that the world of magic and of love that I secretly believed in was all around me, a part of me and a part of what it is to be human. As terrifying as it was to believe, as much as believing felt like dangling upside down from the branch of a tree, I knew the time had come to surrender to the truth that I have the power to conjure what my soul longs for most.

The moral flip side to this story is "Be careful what you wish for." Whether or not you believe you have the power to call things forth in your life, you do.

You are doing it right now.

THE HUGGING SAINT

We named ourselves Li and La. Our Hindu studies had given us a fragmented familiarity with Sanskrit. And *lila,* my same-old and I knew, meant Divine play. We thought we would be less conspicuous by introducing ourselves to Amma's devotees as Li and La, sort of like sacred code names for secret agents. Unlike the others in Amma's satsang group who came to sing, pray, and celebrate their guru, La and I were divinity school students assigned to study and document Amma's worship for Diana Eck's Pluralism Project.

La and I met Truth three months before Amma's arrival in Boston the spring before our graduation. Truth, or *Satya* in Sanskrit, held a Mother's Day celebration for Amma in her home outside Cambridge, where she lived with her teenaged son, Contentment. I soon learned that these names were given by Amma and signified a certain level of devotion—a new life, and a new person they had become with her guidance.

Amma refers to herself most often as simply "a crazy girl in love with God." The rest of the world knows her as a modern Hindu saint with rock-star status, who gives an unconventional and controversial form of *darshan*, or encounter with the guru; she hugs. She also gives women what's called the red thread, ordaining them as priests in her temple, which is considered a revolutionary act in India. Amma, whose name means Mother, travels all over the world hugging every person who comes to see her. Many of her devotees understand her to be an incarnation of the Goddess, specifically, the goddess Kali.

As I've already described, Kali's iconography is provocative, to put it mildly. Her icon would be tough on the in-laws: an intriguing, yet perhaps inappropriate mantelpiece for most Western eyes. In some representations Kali is astride her consort Shiva, who is prostrate, erect, and naked save a loincloth or a snake. Kali dons dismembered body parts, wearing, for example, a skirt of arms, a necklace of skulls, and severed heads for earrings.

The fierceness of Kali's iconography is a symbolic attempt to capture the intensity of her force. The complete transformation Kali's unconditional love demands feels as terrifying as her appearance. It's a love that is powerful and paradoxical, transformational and frightening, because it asks for nothing less than complete surrender.

The satsang, or ceremony to sing praises and love poems to the Divine, took place before an altar in Truth's basement. Amma's image was surrounded by close to a hundred devotees; it was a cramped yet intimate calling-out.

Air suffused with devotion is a strange viscosity to breathe. Devotion to Amma smelled like sandalwood and entered the nostrils as if a thicker element than air. I inhaled deeply among her devotees and could taste an essence of milk, a trace of honey, and a sweetness like coconut.

I have always been easily intoxicated by worship, by the raw displays of devotion it evokes. I thought about all the places, times, and varying traditions that had caused me to swoon with emotion. As I participated in the devotion of Amma as Kali that day at Truth's, I realized why this was the case for me. The woman beside me was Jewish, the man on bent knees behind me Muslim. A common faith was not the unifying force at this gathering; the common thread was love.

As the harmonium began to play and a cacophany of voices began to chant the Goddess's innumerable names, I surveyed the room inconspicuously, marveling at the inherent poetry in Amma's use of spiritual names. Here in this room, before her altar, Truth was a mother, the chosen one sitting next to me wore bifocals, and Contentment was prone to acne. And Grace, good old Grace, was sitting against the far wall behind everyone else, holding tight to the cymbals, which she chimed, of course, at all the right moments.

Just then, a high-pitched voice cracked while crying out "Amma!" The intensity sent an electric shock soaring up my spine. I focused on a framed picture of Amma's smile placed among the flowers and fruit her devotees had offered on the altar. Her teeth were culver-white against the dark-indigo of her skin.

I thought then of her hug. Unlike any other saint in history, Amma acknowledges the body with her form of darshan, embracing what has been excluded from the Divine. In the love Amma's devotees have for her, here in this inconspicuous space of a household basement, the body and the feminine have found their rightful place among the holy.

When the day came at last for me to meet Amma, I was wearing white for the first time, as her devotees had asked me to, and initially it felt like a lie, because ritual purity and handing power over to a guru are notions I could never wear. But I was ready to surrender to the Divine. I was willing for the white I wore that day to symbolize the white flag I was waving for all to see. It was as if a burner had been jacked up to high that Sunday in May at Truth's home, and now, moments before meeting Amma, there was no place left to hide.

All the places in me that I kept from others and even from myself were forced to the surface in the heat. So rather than the more "saintly" me I had wanted to present to Amma for a hug, I felt like my forehead was serving as a billboard confessional. It felt as though I wore all of who I was right there on my face—the good, the bad, and the ugly.

When it was finally my turn to sit in the darshan line approaching Amma, I looked closely at the people willing to wait hours—even the whole night—just to be held in her embrace. Every possible category of human-kind seemed to be represented, and this made me feel as if all would be accepted, even grimy little outcast me.

At one point, as the line snaked around, it brought me alongside an exhausted-looking mother with her four children. I was sitting closest to her youngest, a little girl who was rebraiding her thin, dark hair and bristling with excitement. After twisting the elastic around the end of the braid, she carefully swept both hands across her head, feeling for any lost strands of hair. Then she tucked in her tiny white tee shirt, which was covered with grape juice stains and frayed at the collar from having been worn so often. She yanked up her fire-red socks, and then began to tug at an enormous hole that exposed her left heel. She kept pulling the ends of the fabric together to see what it would look like if the hole were no longer there.

This is when she noticed I was watching her. She became self-conscious and let her heel peek through the hole again. Then she blushed and looked back at her mother, who was speaking quietly but sharply to the little girl's tough-looking teenaged brother. Watching her, I became pensive and wondered what it would have been like to meet the Goddess when I was a little girl.

Just then, a swami called out at the crescendo of his bhajan over the loudspeakers: "Kali Ma, Kali Ma, Kali Ma!" La, who was right behind me in line, rested her hand softly on my shoulder to help me notice that a huge gap had opened up between me and the person before me.

For some reason my heart was pounding painfully fast. I closed up the line behind an elderly woman perched on a meditation cushion and tried to start the Kali mantra I had been using since college. When I couldn't concentrate, I tried to get back to the feeling of being a calm observer, just witnessing devotees being embraced by a woman they consider to be a saint and the goddess Kali. I reminded myself that this was just "field research" and that I would have to write up this experience in an academic paper before graduation. I was a scholar, I reasoned, not a devotee.

Suddenly, the lights were dimmed and a deep-voiced swami began to give meditation instructions over a microphone he was holding far too close to his mouth. As his lips brushed against the microphone, I whispered to La, "Who knew? Barry White is Hindu!" The swami was now unctuously inhaling and exhaling over the loudspeaker as a demonstration of how to meditate. I straightened my back, folded my legs into the lotus position, and followed the swami's advice with exaggerated accuracy.

So there I was, essentially making fun of one of Amma's swamis, playing around and pretending to meditate, when I suddenly couldn't hear myself anymore. My internal monologue went utterly mute. There was only "Ma . . . Ma . . . Ma" resounding with an electric hum inside my head, in a voice I had never heard before. This should have shocked me or made me anxious, but instead I felt an astounding calm—an entire peace.

My eyes moved to focus on the small, nervous fingers of the little girl, again trying to close the hole in her worn-out sock. I say "my eyes," but it was more as if my eyes were being used. It was as if a vastness, waiting just behind me, had unlatched my head and was using my face like a mask to look through and see this little girl without any of my personal stories to narrow its vision.

I became conscious of a simple, yet desperate and urgent need for this child to be loved. Loved unconditionally.

As the little girl sat up on her knees, next in line to be embraced by Amma, she turned back and smiled timidly at me. Twinkling in her eyes was something like magic or hope—something that seems to be lacking in today's world but is essential for every life, especially for the life of a little girl like this one in fire-red socks with a hole in the heel.

Then all at once, Amma's attendants had me on my knees. They wiped my face with a fistful of Kleenex and with deliberate force, pushed me toward the saint. Amma's rich dark hair had been untied and flowed far past her shoulders. She was wearing a gold-tiered crown and a royal purple sari. The air near her felt charged with static electricity, like the atmosphere just before lightning strikes.

The intensity of Amma's stare returned me behind my eyes. I was nowhere but with her. I wiped my trembling palms against my hips, took a deep breath, and then my face was suddenly pressed into the soft folds of Amma's neck. I inhaled her skin's rose scent. She held my head tight to her cheek as she whispered softly in my ear: "Ma . . . Ma . . . Ma."

Then she took my face in both of her hands and tilted her head from side to side at the sight of the tears that were streaming down my face. She kissed me on either cheek while filling my palm with flower petals and Hershey's Kisses. As I started to walk away from her, I managed to take three steps and then collapsed.

I had recognized her voice.

It was her voice I had heard within me while I waited in line. And as I let this recognition wash over me, accepting it fully, I felt a hot surge of blood race into my heart. My ears rang with its throbbing.

And from within this heat, I felt an exquisite intimacy with the knowledge that Amma's hug had recovered for me. The vastness I knew then was my heart's own. This, I remembered, is what I am meant to do—to fall like this and to love from this unnamed vastness within me.

THE SPINNING

The first time it happened I was only half awake. It was as if I was observing someone else's body in motion. I could see the woman's arms, the way she reached up toward the ceiling and then down again as if generating the propulsion to rotate her torso. I could hear her bare feet shuffle in fast, nearly imperceptible increments as she turned. And I could see the ends of her hair whip across her shoulders as she circled faster and faster. Then slowly I awoke and realized that the spinning woman was me. Immediately, I got dizzy and stopped, because in that moment I remembered that I had no idea how to spin so fast and I was afraid I would black out. I felt nauseous and scared, my head in a vise and my heart a fist pounding hard against my chest.

At the time, I was renting an apartment in a mansion on Rue Cernushi in the 17th district of Paris, to serve as my home base in between trips to various pilgrimage sites. I would prepare here in this all-white loft, unfolding a large, beautiful map of France and the neighboring countries on the carpeted floor and drawing red *x*'s on the places where I wanted to go, like Le Puy, Saintes-Maries-de-la-Mer, and Einsiedeln in Switzerland. I made myself very familiar with Central and Southern France and the train routes I would have to take to reach the wilderness outside Zurich where the Black Madonna of Einsiedeln resides.

The spinning freaked me out for a lot of reasons but mostly because I was alone with it. I didn't know who I could explain it to in English, much less in French. And, I had no idea how to categorize the experience or describe what it was or why I did it. It was out of my control. Like sleepwalking, the spinning was more of an unconscious volition, a physical need that overwhelmed me when I was no longer using my rational mind. What I would have given for a mystic crisis hotline at that time!

It scared me because it made me feel as though anything could happen to me. I began to expect the unexpected. And it scared me because at the apex of it, I reached a place where I no longer existed. That's a strange statement I know. But this is what it felt like. In the center of the spinning, it was as if I receded and was no longer attached to my body as it whirled.

It gets stranger. You know how a tornado has an eye? Well, the spinning, too, had a quiet at its core. My body circled and circled, spinning at a speed that would make me sick if I were fully conscious. Eventually, I would reach a place within that stands perfectly still. The spinning would take me to that innermost place that has never moved and never changes. It felt like my essence.

I had read the mystical poetry of Rumi and was familiar with his whirling dervishes. I knew that spinning was a part of their mystical practice. But what I wanted to know was what it meant in my own life.

Once I stopped fearing it and accepted the simplicity of its presence, the spinning no longer happened unexpectedly. My body was simply showing me how it wanted to pray. This was a spiritual practice, a mystical experience that included the body rather than transcended it. It still happens sometimes but now only when I want it to. I think it just wanted me to acknowledge the deep need I had for its medicine—for the healing it could give me every time I surrendered to it.

In losing myself every time I dance, I find the Divine. No matter where I am or who I'm with, I have an all-access pass to the sacred. All I need to do is trust that these holy hands and feet of mine know the way.

The Black Madonna of Einsiedeln

I made the sign of the cross, or tried to, out of reverence and a desire to acknowledge the solemnity of the place. Holy water was dripping from my fingertips. My curiosity forced me to taste it, but I was immediately self-conscious. I looked around quickly to see if anyone had noticed. With the holy water's dusty taste still on my tongue, I walked toward the back wall of the cathedral. The wall was covered with expressions of gratitude from people the Black Madonna of Einsiedeln had healed. Metal sheets had been hammered thin to serve as canvases that held tiny scenes of the miraculous: a woman standing up from her wheelchair, a bedridden man sitting up with a look of astonishment that his prayers at last had been answered. The captions were written in German, but my imagination could interpret the faith each piece of art meant to convey.

I had not anticipated the black obsidian. And I would not have sucked in air so loudly if I knew it would cause half the people sitting near me to whip their heads around and stare. But when I turned from the far wall to face the Black Madonna of Einsiedeln, she stunned me. Her gaze hit me with a force—a blow to the chest—that drew the breath from my body. I had seen her image before, yet pictures of her can't replicate the immensity of her presence. Or at least, that's what I felt when I stood before her for the first time. An impulse swept me from being an art admirer near the far wall to a sudden pilgrim on my knees.

I found myself in the front pew, and I wanted to be closer still. I wanted to enter her temple. She is installed in an inner sanctum made of jet-black obsidian. The rest of the sanctuary is gaudy, with a pastels-and-frosting decor more suited to a baroque wedding cake than a cathedral. But the obsidian of the Black Madonna's temple is austere and exudes a haunting beauty. Set against the peach-and-cream-colored embellishments around it, the temple appears to be the only thing that truly exists in the place.

The cloudlike billows of gold that surround the Black Madonna like a full-body halo seemed protean, evershifting. It looked soft and malleable, as if my fingertip would leave an impression if I touched it. Unless I stared directly at it, the clouds of gold seemed to move around her from the corner of my eye as if its need to radiate could defy chemistry.

The Black Madonna of Einsiedeln wears hand-crafted vestments embroidered with roses. She is laden with jewels, even earrings. She looks both stoic and compassionate, aloof and fiercely present. The child in her lap has a bird perched on his hand. She holds him in a way that makes it immediately evident that he is hers. *This is my son,* her posture declares. *He is of my body.*

My first thoughts were of the wood beneath the Madonna's clothing. I knew that underneath the royal-looking raiments, she was carved. Although I marveled at the adornments, I longed to see the simplicity of the natural wood she was made of. I longed to see the earthiness, the humanity of the icon.

She is a piece of wood, I thought to myself, amazed. *She is a part of the wilderness, the Finsterwald. Why am I here? Why have I been kneed again?*

I began to think then of the belief that angels descend from above. This reinforces the idea that the Divine is something beyond or outside, higher than or superior to the human. I had been thrown off for years by this idea. But in this moment, in the Madonna's gaze, there was no distance, no duality. There was no heaven and earth. There was just this being here, just the pew's hardness against my knees and a fullness of being nowhere but in my skin.

I became aware then of what my soul-voice had been repeating from the moment I turned to face the Black Madonna: "How can I love you more?"

At first, I didn't hear a response. I heard only silence as the question continued to repeat itself deep within me. An elderly man seated in my row stood up, then genuflected, made the sign of the cross, kissed his fingertips, and left. Someone coughed. A child near the far wall, opposite the Black Madonna's temple, laughed. I opened my eyes and focused on the votive candles struggling to stay lit against the cold draft.

My head tilted forward toward my chest. I could see that tears had fallen from my cheeks onto my skin. I admired the precious devotion evident in the folds of my clasped hands. I could see the uncomplicated love of my body. I could see through the thoughts I had of love and witness the raw presence of it in me. I saw the indispensable and elemental aspect of my being, unmasked and unrefined. And it was love. It was the love that had always been and always will be—love enough. I lacked nothing.

As a pilgrim without realizing it, I often repeated one particular phrase while walking along the street. In the evenings when I asked my soul-voice what I needed most to discover, I wrote this phrase in red ink in my journal: *love, true love, means no longer waiting.*

I had no clue what it meant—until, that is, the moment I bowed before the Black Madonna in her obsidian temple in the Finsterwald of Switzerland. The Madonna answered then, and her answer surfaced within me like the small white pupil in the thick dark substance of a Magic 8 Ball: "Love me more by loving you more fully."

And then I felt the riddle I had been repeating to myself suddenly unlock. Love, true love, means no longer waiting. The simple fact that I have a love that makes me capable of risking everything—this is the Divine of my human body.

I lifted my head to look above the Black Madonna, above the billowing clouds of gold surrounding her, past the pointed tips of the golden arrows fanned out around her. I could see then the unpolished raw gold in the shape of a melted heart displayed on the wall in a glass box above the Madonna's alcove. As soon as I saw the golden flames shooting out of the heart, as soon as I saw the misshapen form of what happens when the heart surrenders to its own heat, I knew. I knew that I had come here simply to harness my life to what my heart desires, to what exists most intensely within me.

A heart on fire is not a pretty picture. The heart above the Madonna's alcove was close to gruesome. But a heart engulfed in flames serves as a metaphor. The heat, the spiritual fire generated from the union of body and soul, provides a mirrorlike image of the Divine. This is what levels all being; this is where transcendence and immanence meet. This is what tore the angels from their high and lofty places in my mind, ephemeral and far-reaching, and brought them down to earth where we are eye to eye.

The notion of the human as "lowly" is myopic. Waiting until we are "good enough" is a time that doesn't exist. The condition of being enough is always now, always right here, just requiring our embodiment, our presence, in order for us to truly begin.

Teresa of Avila, in the *Interior Castle,* calls the room where the Divine dwells within the soul "another heaven." The form of vision that can perceive this room is the same vision the Apostles used to encounter Jesus. He appeared within them suddenly, Teresa writes, "without entering through the door."[2]

The alchemists worshiped something known as "the wingless bird," or fiery red sulfur. Marie-Louise von Franz defines this as "the active part of the psyche, the part that has a definite goal."[3] The red wingless bird is related to desire, ambition, and the power drive. "It is an underlying factor of the inner psychic life and is always what one has first to unearth,"[4] she tells us. For me, this red wingless bird flew toward one goal: revealing my soul.

When the soul can be perceived in the body, the outcome is "mercurius," according to the alchemists. Mercurius is the Divine child, "the symbol of a new, objective attitude beyond conflict,"[5] and, according to von Franz, the Divine child is born in "the philosopher's egg," or "sealed alchemical vessel."[6] When meeting the soul or the unconditional love the soul contains, something new is inexorably born.

This birth, this newfound life within me, changed me in the following way: I could hear my soul-voice with ease and not just in meditation. This is explained by von Franz as "the Self [soul] becoming immediate," which "is the same thing as being completely natural and instinctive, when one can discern between the false and the true."[7]

In alchemical language, the immediate awareness of the soul is the longed-for thing. This is our ultimate goal and treasure. This is the philosopher's stone.[8] To describe this process, von Franz cites the ancient symbol of the Ouroboros—a giant serpent with its own tail in its mouth: one becomes like this "tail-eater" through meeting the Divine within. By connecting to what before was "other," by becoming whole, "there is a flow born, which is what the alchemists mean by the mystical or divine water."[9]

While I was inside the Cathedral of the Black Madonna of Einsiedeln, the rain stopped, and when I pushed open the large wooden door of the main sanctuary, I breathed in the fresh wet smell of leaves and pavement. Just outside the cathedral entrance, there is a fountain with 13 small waterspouts surrounding the statue of a woman wearing a crown of stars. That morning, I had bought two small plastic bottles with a picture of the Black Madonna of Einsiedeln on the side. As I was filling them with water from the fountain, I looked up at the statue and thought how beautiful she was and how perfectly situated. The stars encircling her head are as golden as the billowing clouds surrounding the Black Madonna inside. But this woman is outside the cathedral, with the elements, in a story that she has penned herself.

I raised one of the little bottles of water in the air as if toasting the memory of the great 16th-century alchemist Paracelsus. Einsiedeln was his birthplace. I repeated his well-known motto, *Alterius non sit qui suus esse potest,* which translates as "Let no one who can belong to [herself] belong to another." I took a sip.

Saint Augustine, in his spiritual memoir, *Confessions,* says that what he longed for, what he traveled far and wide to find, was the presence he could only at last embrace within: "And see, you were within and I was in the external world and sought you there, and in my unlovely state I plunged into those lovely created things which you made. You were with me, and I was not with you."[10]

Though the external world pulled Augustine, nothing external to him compared with the divinity of his own being: "You called and cried out loud and shattered my deafness . . . You were fragrant, and I drew in my breath and now pant after you . . . You touched me, and I am set on fire to attain the peace which is yours."[11]

Augustine later confesses that this mystical experience of meeting the Divine, the beauty of a love so old and so new, demonstrates to him that "a body by its weight tends to move towards its proper place."[12] Just as oil poured under water is drawn up to the surface of the water, and likewise water poured on top of oil sinks below the oil, each is only acting in accordance with its own density. "They seek their own place,"[13] he explains. I understood then that love is my weight. Wherever I had been led and wherever I would then be carried, it was the love in my soul that led me, it was my soul that ordered my world and my priorities.

THE MOST STRANGE

As a little girl, I pretended I had special powers. I could heal people by saying words over their bodies. They couldn't see this, but the words were actually visible to me. They were gold and sparkly, and as they fell onto someone's body, they dissolved into a liquid that looked like honey. I imagined flying from city to city, healing people invisibly as they slept. I lived in a tall tree with an impossibly thick trunk and roots that extended down to the center of the earth. It had branches like strong arms that held me and huge lavender blooms that calmed me. I had innumerable adventures and encountered malevolent forces and tyrants that wanted to harm the people I loved, but I always saved the day—and always before dinner was ready.

In my experience, my imagination didn't just disappear one day along with my imaginary friends. It somehow got rerouted from being a source of renewal, adventure, and inspiration to being a tool for dread. By the time I was a teenager, if I was worried about something, my imagination would help me conjure the most terrifying outcome. Or it would help convince me that there were burglars on the roof rather than two cats mating. (I was so certain of this once that I called the police.) I saw a snake rather than the garden hose.

My imagination was in the service of fear.

I was doped up on more Ativan than any human, three times my weight, should consume. And yet still, somehow, I was conscious, drooling slightly, but conscious. It was the week before Christmas in 2001. I took a train from Paris to London in order to travel to the U.S. with my sister. War was underway; it was time to go home.

So the scene was much the same as on Flight U.S. Scare. My sister was beside me in the window seat, and I was drenched with anxiety, gasping at any noise or tremor the airplane made. There was also a baby screaming like in the 13 nightmares. She was in the seat across the aisle, but I couldn't look at her. I had enough chaos of my own to contend with. It took all my concentration to keep the tug-of-war between love and fear going on inside me stacked in love's favor. If love lost, I felt certain I would do something categorically insane and have to be injected with the knockout serum I've always imagined they keep on board for just such occasions.

The low point was when for some never-explained reason the whole cabin went pitch dark. My heart dislodged from my chest and seemed to beat against the back of my throat. Sheer panic fire-worked out of every nerve ending. The blackout probably lasted half a minute at most, but those seconds were each experienced as timeless, individual moments. *Here it is,* I thought, *this is the second right before we plummet.* And then, when for once I didn't let fear pull a rip cord and send me straight out of my body, here's what I felt: love. When the worst possible outcome I could imagine was unfolding, I felt love. It overwhelmed fear with its reality.

When the imagination is called back in the service of love, we recover one of our most powerful spiritual tools. We can use imagination as we did when we were little, to remind us that we are never alone, that we are capable of anything, and that miracles are a part of everyday life, like toast and slippers and taking out the garbage. When we allow ourselves to be surrounded by what love believes, our lives are mystically drenched and spiritually pregnant with all the magical beings and happy endings we could ever hope for. This, I realized, was the spiritual tool I had been missing on Flight U.S. Scare—the capacity to connect with the reality of love when fear is blaring its alarm through every cell in my body.

The lights turned back on, and the red Fasten Your Seat Belt Sign was turned off. All was well. As we neared the eastern coast of the United States, I started to let myself trust that we were actually going to land. I released my sweaty grasp on the armrests and flexed my hands. I let my body feel what it's like to fly without tension. Then I darted a glance in the baby's direction.

It was a little girl. She had stopped crying and was arching her back on her mother's lap, trying to reach the floor and test out her new feat of walking. Her mother stood and tried to take her hand, but the child shot off down the aisle with a drunken-sailor walk, while squealing in those high pitches only babies can manage. Her little baby hair was standing on end from static, the top of her head just barely visible above the armrests. I kept my eyes on her as she reached the end of our aisle, then turned and came running back toward my seat.

Looking at her was all the invitation she needed to come barreling up to me. She held onto my leg with both of her chunky, dimpled hands, while her mother apologized profusely. Then she lifted up her shirt to press her belly button, I think in an effort to impress me. And then she slid her shirt back down and held the hem out as if for me to read the message on the front on her shirt in case I had missed it, which I had.

In big capital letters across her chest it said LOVE.

I know; it's trite. The shirt was no doubt from Baby Gap. Something like that is the simplest thing in the world to dismiss. The little details always are. But the only thing that matters is the experience of it, not the forethought or afterthought or any thought in between. It would be so much safer to remain in the glass box of disbelief. I would never be exposed to ridicule that way. But I would also miss out on how intoxicating it feels to have everything around me conspiring to return me to love.

In *On Love and Other Difficulties,* Rilke suggests that "perhaps all the dragons of our lives are princesses who are only waiting to see us once beautiful and brave. Perhaps everything terrible is in its deepest being something helpless that wants help from us."[14] Humankind must expect existence to contain the possibility of everything, including, or especially, the most "un-heard-of,"[15] he says. But the miraculous and the unheard of take courage to expect and to see and to not discount once they happen. This, Rilke suggests, is the only real courage that is demanded of us: "to have courage for the most strange, the most singular, and the most inexplicable that we may encounter."[16]

KNOW THYSELF

Encountering the Divine, experiencing life as mystical in our own ways, in our own lives, inspires us, renews us, and reminds us again and again that everything is still possible. It brings hope. It prevents burnout. It allows our imagination to flourish with deep green verdure and to hum with the creatures and magical beings we once made room for at the dinner table.

I have revealed myself as a freelance mystic, or what the writer and teacher Caroline Myss calls "a mystic without a monastery." I have gotten spiritually naked in this chapter because I know I am not alone. I know just how many of us long to exist mystically, to not just talk about the Divine but encounter the sacred right here in our human bodies and daily lives. We still have the remnants of a third eye, the eye of insight. But we have to pull it back from ages of atrophy and practice its use, to make it as functional and as real as the two eyes you are using to read this.

The capacity to perceive the Divine has to be cultivated. Mysticism is not a luxury; it's a necessity. The mystical is not elusive, or exclusive to the spiritual elite. We all have encounters with the sacred. We just have to cultivate the eye that can perceive them. We have to see what's already here, interwoven with what we claim is human and mundane. We have to take inventory of the magic that conspires to love us in and through our ordinary lives.

I think that so many of us still fear being fully present in the body because it means owning just how powerful we are. The responsibility is overwhelming. We then enter a place where we are held accountable for what we really know. We have an immediate sense of what is true for us. Real courage is simply surrendering to that. There's nothing more powerful than a woman who has met the truth inside her. Nothing.

Knowing the self means knowing the soul.

Lift the veil that shrouds your strangeness. Dare to see how powerful you are.

The Sixth Veil

REVEAL Your Soul-Work

There is a vitality, a life force, an energy, a quickening that is translated through you into action, and because there is only one of you in all of time, this expression is unique. And if you block it, it will never exist through any other medium and it will be lost.

—MARTHA GRAHAM

THE FUNNY PART

You are here to love.

The ending is just the beginning.

Once we have met with the limitless love of the soul, we begin again, begin anew.

Over the past decade, in the wake of recession and war, there has been a boom of women stepping up to claim their soul-work in the world. With profound clarity and creativity, the new Rosie the Riveter is an entrepreneur, a spiritual activist, a wellness warrior, a REVEALer, finding her unique and authentic way of being in service to the world.

Soul-work can be volunteer, supplemental, or full-time. It is work that doesn't take you away from your life; it's work that doesn't feel like work at all. It's not separate from who you are; it fits seamlessly. It's not an occupation; it's your soul's vocation. We are all, lay and ordained alike, called to do something that shares the deep medicine the soul contains.

Soul-work is not about martyrdom. The vision of sainthood that demands lack and deprivation is no longer useful. Soul-work is about Divine reciprocity in which the love you give is the love you receive in equal measure. You know you are doing your soul-work in the world if you feel that you are receiving as much as you are giving.

And with soul-work, giving comes from a place of overflowing. We don't give and give and give to the point of being dried up, burned out, and empty. We've been there, tried that. It serves no one. You allow love to nourish you. You give from a place of being abundantly filled with love from within. You meet others' needs from a place of already having met every single one of your own.

Soul-work may not look "soulful" at all. Delete the images you might have of being in a foreign country, feeding the poor. That's a nice image, but it might not be true for you. I have had professions that elicited tons of accolades and praise. They were the expected forms of work that someone who is spiritual would do. My work with emotionally disturbed children and pregnant teens was good work, and life-altering lessons were gleaned, but did I truly share myself? No, and I felt it. I couldn't receive the praise and support I got for doing such "good, hard work." There was a holy restlessness, a palpable sense of knowing that this may be good work, inspiring even, but it wasn't what my soul was pressing me on to do.

Finding soul-work can feel like walking forward while wearing a blindfold. The key is to trust what your soul-voice is telling you. It plays a sacred game of hot and cold as you get nearer or further from the work that will truly reveal you. Soul-work is not something you can identify from your ego's sense of being impressed. An increased sense of feeling important is a distraction, a red flag.

All that matters is that your work humbles you and reminds you that the evolution of the soul is never-ending. All that matters is that you feel that incomparable exalted state of knowing that you have done what you came here to do. Soul-work is only inwardly recognizable. It is the work that expands your capacity to love. It is the work that asks you to become more love in order to complete it.

The funny part is that it's all so simple. What we are meant to do is who we are. Nothing more. Our soul-work is merely an extension of our own essence. It just takes such an effort for so many of us to get that naked. To simply let what we do be who we are.

THE HAPPY FLOOR

All I could do was focus on the coffee stain that was slowly spreading across her white, wrinkled shirt. The energy that was radiating out of her body overpowered her words. In my memory, during that whole first moment of our encounter, her speech was on mute. Her fear and her anger drowned out any words with an electric intensity.

Regardless of what she actually said to me, what I heard was this: "I am afraid, and I hate you. I hate you because I hate God. I hate you because I'm terrified you are going to try to tell me that God is still good. My niece is dead, and her twin died last week. There is no God. So don't you dare stand there and try to suggest that there still might be good in this world."

The Neonatal Intensive Care Unit at New York–Presbyterian Hospital functioned like a delicately balanced ecosystem. I always imagined that the isolettes, the feeding tubes, and the wires that snaked their way all over the room to monitor those impossibly small hearts were evidence of a complex root system that inextricably connected each of the preemies on the NICU to each other.

When one of those tiny bodies stopped breathing, it didn't feel like one life had ended. It felt to the rest of the NICU as if a whole world, a whole universe, had been lost. The impact was nothing short of catastrophic for the entire floor. Each time there was a tiny last breath, the fabric of reality seemed to shift. We all felt it. And as the NICU chaplain, it was my job to somehow rein in the ensuing chaos.

When I first interviewed for a position as a chaplain at the hospital, I requested the Labor and Delivery floor. The supervisor of the clinical pastoral education department laughed and said, "That's the happy floor. We don't have chaplains assigned there."

My face fell. My voice dropped. "The happy floor?" I questioned, with my eyebrow raised for emphasis. The supervisor was gracious, a Presbyterian minister. He waved his hand just slightly as if to suggest that by all means, go ahead, let 'er rip.

"*Ecstatic, life-altering, traumatic, spiritual, exhilarating, terrifying, unforgettable,* and *indescribable* are words I hear about childbirth, but *happy?* Never," I told him. "I have never heard that word used by a mother in labor." I could feel a rash zigzagging its way up my neck from the passion that had seized me in that moment.

I told him about my background in feminist theology and my training as a doula, a labor coach, before entering seminary. I needed this position to fulfill field education credits for my Master of Divinity degree. I was confident there was a large unmet need on the L & D ward for a spiritual presence to provide support and a sense of the sacred for many women who experience childbirth as one of life's greatest transitions, second only to death.

He agreed. His one condition was that I also become the chaplain of the NICU. I agreed.

I was part of a cadre of chaplains, except that they all had particular traditions that they represented within the hospital. I was asked if I wanted to be Wiccan or Interfaith, and I said no thanks. Had there been a chaplain of Mary Magdalene's lineage, I would have worn the label proudly on my lapel.

We were each assigned to different floors or units of the hospital. Patients were usually informed about the hospital's chaplaincy services by their doctors at particularly hard moments of their treatment. Sometimes we were called by nursing staff for emotional assistance when a death or a dark diagnosis loomed.

I was paged constantly throughout the day, and most often it was to come to the NICU. Once the nursing staff understood that I wasn't spewing scripture or interested in stealthily converting anyone to a particular sect, they called on me to help quiet the emotional maelstroms that occurred when a preemie was born or at a preemie's death.

This is how I found myself suddenly standing in front of the woman with the coffee stain who hated me with every cell in her body, amalgamating her anger for the hospital, for God, and for life itself into a force that hit me square in the solar plexus. I was flushed from the intensity of her emotions. The nurse was waving for me to usher the family into the small holding room on the NICU where the three-pound body of her niece was waiting. I can still see the exaggerated way the nurse motioned for me, fueled by her own stress from the loss of her most recent patient. If her body could have spoken to me in that moment it would have said, "Get a move on it, you sensitive freak. Get this family away from the other families before all hell breaks loose."

There are no words at such moments. We should have sign language for tragic moments like the death of a baby. We shouldn't have to use words. Words are stiff and limited. I wanted to be able to just speak with my eyes, with my hand on the center of the woman's back. I wanted to be able to just be there with her in her grief, acknowledging the devastation and nothing more.

The nurse waved her Bingo arm at me furiously one more time. I suggested to the grieving aunt that it might feel significant to say good-bye. I let her know that the rest of the family was waiting for her in the room at the center of the NICU. She shot eye-daggers at me and then stormed off in the direction of her niece's body.

I experienced many deaths on the NICU over the course of the year I served as a chaplain. But this death was the most painful. I felt unable to provide solace to this family, a family I wanted to reach out to the second I met with their inconsolable suffering.

Chaos won out that day.

On the bus ride home, I sat in the back and lost it. I didn't care who saw me. I curled forward and bawled. I kept seeing that oblong coffee stain. I kept feeling the raw, disorienting pain the family felt. At the news of the second death, the second twin lost, their lives no longer made sense. I felt all of this. I understood. But I had failed to be there—to find a way to suggest that love still exists, that their pain is love. The immensity of their emotion was the presence of love. As brief as their lives had been, those two tiny girls had exponentially increased their family's capacity to love. And this enlarged capacity to love in each of them will remain for the rest of their lives. This was the undying gift the twins had given.

Then the inevitable came: I judged myself. Big-time. I sucked at chaplaincy. Who was I kidding to think I fit in? To think I might have found a spiritual home? I took off the security badge that I wore around my neck all day as if removing a medal from a disqualified athlete. I had hit bottom. I closed my eyes.

That's when a flood of images came to me. In the soft, open space of silence and humility that follows defeat, I saw flashes of the women I had been able to serve as a chaplain. I saw the terror in Lupe's eyes when she was told she would need a C-section before her husband could arrive. I saw myself scramble to find a translator so

I could describe the procedure to her and alleviate her fear. I saw the flood of love, gratitude, and relief in her eyes when she emerged from surgery; she grasped my hand so tightly it hurt.

I saw Annabelle in her bed, weary from the stress of needing to stay in bed on the antepartum floor for months before her twin sons were born. I could see the fear in her face, communicating with ease what she couldn't bring herself to verbally express: the sense of feeling ineffectual, useless, and unproductive. I had seen that look so many times.

"It's so easy to forget," I told her with a smile.

"Forget what?" she said, slightly annoyed but intrigued nonetheless.

"It's easy to forget that while you're sitting here doing nothing, your body is ceaselessly forming two human lives."

I remembered her face transforming from frustration to pure joy.

I saw us meeting each week to visualize that her sons were both head down, ready for a healthy vaginal delivery. Every day we prayed this way, seeing together what she wanted to come true, not what she feared might happen. We held hands as she closed her eyes to speak to them, to tell them how much she already loved them.

I saw the tears streaming down her cheeks in the hallway on the postpartum floor on the morning when her boys finally came, born in the exact way she had imagined.

I saw Rivka with her wire-rimmed glasses reflecting the red flashing lights above her son's isolette. He was seven hours old, he weighed one pound, and a bevy of doctors and nurses were crowding around his tiny baby-bird body as it went code blue. Her wheelchair was set back from the mayhem. She had one hand in her lap as if holding the incision of her recent C-section and the other holding tight to her IV pole. This was the only emotion she allowed herself in that moment—the white-knuckled grip on the metal pole. From the moment I saw her, from the moment I met with her raw courage and profoundly unassuming bravery, I wanted to do everything and anything I could to give to her somehow, to be of use to her in her pain.

This was Rivka's 11th child. She was 47 years old and a member of a Hasidic community on Manhattan's Upper West Side. I had been informed by the Jewish chaplain on staff that because of the insular nature of her community, she would probably not acknowledge me even if I addressed her directly. So when she asked me for a cup of ice, I was elated. I raced down the hallway to the nurse's station to get Rivka her ice. If this was all I could do, I would be grateful.

But I got to do far more. Every time Rivka's son made some small yet tremendous step toward survival, she would come to find me. She would tell me with such pride and love things like "He took his first breath on his own today"; "He has gained a whole pound"; "He opened his eyes." I had the honor of being her witness. And I got to respond to her with words that my soul hinted she had never heard before in her life, comments like "Your love for him is miraculous"; "You are a warrior"; "Your strength is holy."

I saw myself weaving in and out of the rooms on the NICU, sensing where I was needed most. Often before the call even came through on my beeper, I was there.

I was there to lead a couple through a ritual to say good-bye to their baby. Chills raced through me as the father placed his hand on the perfect dome of his little girl's head to bless her for having been with him, if only for one day. I was there to give a blessing to a couple leaving with their glowing baby boy, who squirmed and squealed in my arms as I asked that he find his way in this world always surrounded and guided by love. I was there as a part of the delicate ecosystem of those impossibly small hearts and incalculably large souls.

As I sat there bobbing along in the backseat of the crosstown bus, I realized that for the first time in my life I knew happiness not as an ideal or a concept but as an actual state of being. Happiness wasn't something external, out there, remote and unattainable. Happiness was an actual sensation I could locate in my body. Like a bone or a major organ, happiness was a part of my physical presence. I was happy—and it wasn't the fleeting kind of happiness that relies on something or someone else to maintain it. I had found a stable, bedrock kind of happiness, and here's why: every gift that existed within me was called upon.

I had found my own definition of happiness; I had tasted it. Happiness comes when all that I am is being utilized. Happiness comes when what exists within me is being shared. Happiness is being aware of the gift of love I possess and then getting blessed with the opportunity to give it away.

Not This, Not That

Apophatic theology, or *via negativa* (Latin for "negative way"), attempts to understand and speak about the

Divine by describing what the Divine is not. Within the Eastern Orthodox Church, apophatic theology is based on the assumption that the essence of the Divine cannot be defined or understood in any human language.

Hinduism shares a similar analytical process called *neti neti,* Sanskrit for "not this, not that." Neti neti is used to describe the ineffable vastness of Brahma (the Divine) by saying what Brahma is not, since in the end, there is no description, no metaphor, no string of perfectly crafted words that can express what cannot in fact be adequately captured in any language.

The path to find my soul-work in the world was one of the via negativa. I had to go through a lot of neti neti before I found the work that revealed my soul—the desire to share what was within me demanded it. For example, I wanted to be a chaplain. Badly. But certification would necessitate that I choose a particular religious tradition to represent. There was no going further up and further in if I didn't have an organized and institutionalized spirituality that could support, monitor, and validate my work.

I meditated a deep groove into my wood floors during that time. I wanted so desperately to hear *yes, it's ok, go ahead and return to the Unitarian Church. Become a minister even,* I tried to arm-wrestle my soul-voice into saying. But that's not what I heard. What I heard was, *your one true ministry is love.*

Great. Thanks. And my salary will come from . . . ?

Neti neti is ultimately about discernment—"delicate discrimination." It is the art of seeing clearly, of piercing through obscurity and knowing which way is not necessarily the "right" way according to anyone else but is the only way our own soul is telling us to go.

Discernment can be difficult. Often there's a lot of spiritual sweat involved, because we're not ready to see what, in fact, the soul is clearly showing us we need to do. We create aversions and distractions, and we flail around as if we're drowning, or we pretend that we're lost. Lost is a comforting place to be; we don't have to do anything there but be lost. I know: I chose it many, many times. Being lost lets us hover and gives us the illusion that at least we're not making any mistakes. But lost is a choice. When we're lost, we're not engaged in life in any way, so there's a false sense of freedom.

One of the most profound suggestions I have ever been given about work came from my mom. She suggested that any door would lead me to the right door. I couldn't miss it. I couldn't lose out on what I'm here to do any more than I could lose my own nose. I just needed to make choices, not hover. No matter what I did, I needed to choose to not be lost and to know that wherever I landed with my two feet and abnormally large heart, it was going to lead me to where I needed to be. As long as I was fully present and fully me, I would find my way.

I had a quote from the Gospel of Thomas, one of the Gnostic Gospels found at Nag Hammadi, affixed to the center of a vision board I had made with images that inspired me. In the quote Jesus says, "If you bring forth what is within you, what is within you will save you."[1] The other half of the quote says that if you *don't* bring forth what is within you, it will kill you. For me, this was true. I knew that revealing my soul would save me. I also knew that some part of me would die if I didn't find the way to share what was inside me.

While I was in seminary, I lived in what used to be the convent for Riverside Church, an interdominational church on Manhattan's Upper West Side. My room was at eye level with the stained-glass windows along the nave of the sanctuary narrating Jesus's ministry. Only a courtyard separated me from the Passion of Christ. I felt like a recluse in my small, 333-square-foot apartment. I made use of my time as an urban nun. I meditated in my huge papasan chair, to see if I could reach that state of undiluted love I had experienced while being kneed on the pilgrimage. I didn't want to just be overcome by that state; I wanted to learn how to get there myself. This is when I found the writings of the Desert Fathers, early Christian monastics, and the stories of the hermits known as hesychasts.

Hesychasm is a mystical tradition of experiential prayer among male monastics in the Eastern Orthodox Church that dates back to as early as the 4th century. It's a form of contemplative meditation, of going within that I was initially surprised to find in Christianity, since I thought of meditation as exclusive to Buddhism. Hesychasts focus all their attention in the heart while repeating the Jesus Prayer, an incantation of forgiveness and gratitude for what the Divine has done, is doing, and will continue to do. The repetition of *Kýrie, eléison,* Greek for "Lord, have mercy," is the origin of the Jesus Prayer, which is said to be a prayer that opens the heart.

Just as a lover is always conscious of their beloved, hesychasts reach a state of constant prayer in which they are always conscious of the Divine's presence in their lives. The prayer of the heart is an incessant calling out to the Divine. The hesychast's goal is *theosis,* or union with the Divine. This practice is linked to a passage from the Song of Songs: "I sleep, but my heart is awake."[2]

Rather than sitting up straight like practitioners of Buddhist meditation, hesychasts curl forward over their chests as if this posture can help them center their attention more intensely on the heart. So initially, when I curled forward, I imagined the space of my heart—what it really meant—a limitless space inside.

Sometimes I could sense the presence of my soul, because hot tears would start to roll down my cheeks from the intimacy of being so near to all that undying love. Other times, I heard a word or two, sometimes even a statement, and I would know that it was my soul-voice, because every inch of my body would affirm that it was. I felt that spine-tingling chill that has become a spiritual barometer for me of encountering the Divine. When I graduated from seminary and moved into an apartment, I took my hesychast-inspired, heart-centered practice with me, but I renamed it the soul-voice meditation.

My altar at the time was a discarded hostess stand from a French bistro. I had found it one night on the street—New York City urban renewal at its best. The stand was made of wood with red writing in French along its sides. I turned it so that the opening where the menus had been stored faced into the room. I lined it with red velvet and placed images and icons of Mary Magdalene, Saint Sarah-La-Kali, the Black Madonna, the Hindu goddess Kali, and the Tibetan goddess Tara on the shelf.

Several months before graduation, I meditated for an answer to the question of whether or not I should apply for a doctorate in theology. I barely had time to go within before I heard a resounding "No!" I applied anyway.

The stability I imagined I would have as a professor was too alluring.

So there I was, rejection letter in hand, not a chaplain, not a would-be professor, not a minister, sitting before my makeshift altar, bent forward over my heart, when I heard my soul-voice repeat a portion of that quote from the Gospel of Thomas: *"What is within you will save you."*[3] I finally allowed myself to take ownership of what I had always sensed: I was never going to find a spiritual home.

I had to bring it out from within me.

THE LIST AND FINDING LUCKY

I prayed all the time and anywhere: on the subway, waiting in line at the grocery store, while swimming laps in the pool. Prayer became an experience, an emotion, a state of being I could willfully enter into without anyone knowing. I didn't have to physically curl forward over my heart; I didn't have to be sitting on a cushion in front of my altar. The lit candle, the silent and reverent place where my soul could whisper to me or just slap my face to wake me up was always right there with me wherever I went—in my heart.

This meeting with my soul replaced my long-standing practice of reciting the List. Prayer for me used to look like this: I sat down somewhere very quiet, most often before my altar. I lit a candle, I lit incense, and I quieted my mind. I noticed any negative thoughts that needed ousting, and then I started the List. I would name, one by one, all the things that I wanted in my life.

For years, I had been longing to meet my Tall, Dark, and Handsome. And by my early 30s, my biological clock had been going off for about a decade, its shrill alarm always present. I often felt lonely or sad, as if I was missing my T, D, and H and the baby I hadn't yet had. So at the top of the List was my longing for a true love in my life. Our love baby came next. Then I usually mentioned financial abundance (so I could afford the baby) and some sort of gorgeous apartment or home (so I had a place to raise the baby). The List had existed for as long as I could remember, incessantly calling out all those intangible and material things I wanted most. I repeated ad nauseam all the things I lacked in my life. And guess what? I kept getting exactly that: lack.

This is the greatest gift the prayer of the heart gave me. When I was fully present in my heart, there was no room for what I was missing. There was just the beauty of being met fully. I lacked nothing. My List went blank. Rather than focus on the feeling of what I didn't have— the man, the baby, the home—I started cultivating the feeling of already having everything I need.

One of my REDLADIES had given me three little bamboo shoots that we had named Lucky. I decided to love the hell out of Lucky. I said hello and good-bye to him whenever I went out or came home. I set him next to me while I ate dinner alone. I talked to him, asked him how his day went. And whenever sadness for a family of my own crept in, I reminded myself that I had Lucky in my life.

Everything on the List came—but only after I had let it go.

DOING NOTHING

When I saw Liam Neeson's hand go up, my anxiety struck a large gong inside me; I could hardly stand still from the reverberations. I steadied myself on the desk, my desk, and answered every other parent's question in the hopes he would put his hand down in the meantime. He didn't. I finally nodded in his direction and prayed that I could respond to him without accidentally allowing my jaw to drop at his excessive beauty. I've never trusted myself less. He began speaking, but all I could think was *Holy crap, Qui-Gon Jinn from* The Phantom Menace *is asking me a question.* I was freaking out so loudly inside I had to squint in an effort to concentrate and actually hear what he was saying.

He asked me an articulate and relevant question about the fact that the curriculum I had created for the 7th grade World Religions class did not include a section on atheism and agnosticism. I was amazed that I responded at all. I can't remember what I said, but I know I went on for far too long and didn't even come close to answering his question.

Thankfully, the master teacher who had been assigned to help me learn how to translate my theological lexicon into language a 7th grader could understand had the wisdom to be there with me that night. She cut in on my verbal train wreck and answered Mr. Neeson like a normal, functioning human being.

There were two doors to my classroom. When the parent-teacher conference was over, I shook hands with several of the parents, relieved that I had made it through the evening without passing out. Then from the corner of my eye, I saw that Qui-Gon Jinn was leaning against the door frame as if he was waiting for some-one. I assumed it was for me. (Of course, he could have been waiting for anyone in the room, a notion that only occurred to me once I got back home.) My response—I bolted out the other door.

By this point, I read my life the way I read my dreams—symbolically. Too many synchronicities had happened for me to ignore the evidence that curious en-counters are in my life to teach me something. For me, encountering Qui-Gon Jinn had everything to do with the greatest lesson I became a 7th grade World Religions teacher to learn: Doing Nothing. I had to work my as-sets off in a private all-boys' middle school to learn the delicate art of effortless action. This is what Qui-Gon Jinn would call the Force, and what Taoism would call Wu Wei.

In order to help make Wu Wei more comprehensible to my class, I assigned Benjamin Hoff's *The Tao of Pooh*. Wu Wei, according to Lao Tzu, the founder of Taoism, pertains to the art of knowing when to act and when not to. It is a feminine way of being in the world that re-quires the ego to submit and allows for the natural flow of the universe to unfold.

The literal meaning of Wu Wei is "without action, without effort, without control." It's a state of effort-lessly doing what needs to be done. It contains the para-dox of acting in such balance and harmony with the universe that there's no actual action at all. It is just a sense of allowing the perfect equilibrium of the universe to establish itself through you.

The aim is to align yourself with the Tao (or the Force, if you prefer) in order to acquire a form of malleable and invisible power. It's a power that at first seems weak or submissive, like water flowing the way the current directs. And yet, the combination of the water's flexibility and the current's strength creates epic wonders naturally. Yes, think Grand Canyon.

Winnie-the-Pooh personifies the philosophy of Wu Wei. Somehow, without Pooh even trying, everything turns out perfectly for him. No matter what comes his way, he doesn't get caught up in making something more complex than it is, the way Owl does, and he doesn't become fearful or pessimistic like Eeyore. Pooh just lets everything be, controls nothing, and inevitably comes out of every situation on top.

This Taoist feminine principle of effortless action illuminated what already existed in my life. It gave me the capacity to see what had already come to me without effort and enabled me to distinguish between what I had to do and what I thought I wanted to do in the world. I learned to resist nothing.

What am I talking about?

Compulsion is the state of being compelled, a force that compels, or a persistent, irresistible impulse. I became conscious of actions that truly originate from within me, actions that my soul compels me to take. I realized that I had failed to notice what I was already doing, because it felt less like *doing* and more like *being*. It was work I didn't even consider work because it didn't feel like work at all—I *had* to do it, and it sustained me.

"Lighthouses don't go running all over an island looking for boats to save," writer and activist Anne Lamott reminds us. "They just stand there shining."[4] Rather than chase after where I imagined the light might be for me, I stood still and became it. I started right where I was. I took stock of my compulsions: pilgrimages, theology degrees, devouring every fiction or nonfiction book that had to do with the Divine Feminine, and, of course, being kneed. I could see then that the REDLADIES, the small women's spirituality group I had been facilitating since I returned from the pilgrimage ten years ago, is my soul-work. I was providing what I needed most to receive: the spiritual mentorship of women.

This is how I knew I was doing the work of my soul: in order to build my career, I kept meeting the precise challenges that would require me to let go of my ego even more. I practiced my soul-voice meditation as if it were a sacred game of Simon Says. If I heard my soul say "No," I listened, even if it didn't make sense to my rational mind. I let my soul lead. I had been humbled too often to think that I knew the way. I didn't. My soul did.

Day by day and faster than I ever could have imagined, my career as a spiritual mentor or freelance mystic was realized. I had finally learned the sacred feminine art of doing nothing, fiercely loving the ego into submission to allow the soul its sovereignty.

How Women Pray When No One Else Is Watching

I was standing at the podium in front of a sea of women. I was looking down at the words I had typed out to speak, but a raw emotion was washing over me, holding me silent and forcing me to be present to it.

For the first time in my life, I wasn't a spiritual outsider. I was in the presence of my community, my tribe, and my long-lost soul sisters. I was standing at last in my spiritual home. Gratitude was radiating out of me with a force that made my hands shake as I held the pages of my speech. This is when I sobbed unintelligible sobs of joy. I had arrived. My body communicated my profound relief. *I am home,* it told me, *I can stop searching; the pilgrimage is over. This, right here, is what I have been restless to find since I was ten years old.*

After I let my body silently express my gratitude, in response every woman in the audience leapt to her feet and started whistling, woo-hoo-ing, and shouting out her own joy. In that moment, I reveled in the Divine equation that nothing comes to life on its own. We unveil our soul-work to the world not only in the presence of but also because of the love and wisdom of a community. I had never been alone. In some miraculous way, I had always been with these women who were now standing before me. And in retrospect, I adore the visual message that moment gave me—that if a woman dares to stand for the voice of her soul, to follow that soul-voice with fidelity and conviction, there will be a community of women who will stand to join her.

I call this memory the Birth of REVEAL.

At the end of the day, as music filled the air, I flashed on an image of the panel from that morning. A long, rectangular table had been set up on stage with microphones for seven female speakers to talk about their relationship to the Divine Feminine, mysticism, sexuality, the sacredness of their bodies, and the wisdom and power all of us are ready to own. The image made my soul smile, because I had named the memory of that panel, that platform of women claiming their divinity, the First Supper.

And then we danced. All of us. At the end of the day, we shed the weight of ourselves and let our souls come to the surface for some much-needed air. I danced with a woman who had tears streaming down her face, I danced with a woman smiling so widely her face looked broken open, and I danced with a woman so uninhibited, so fully in her body, that I gasped in awe at the beauty of such union.

I danced with every woman, knowing that we were no longer strangers, that we have a community now to support us in the soul-work we long most to do in the world. We don't have to talk about the sacredness of our bodies or prove our innate wisdom. Not now. Now we just celebrate it. As I smiled at each woman I danced with, I heard my soul-voice whisper, *"This is the way women pray when no one else is watching."*

In Tibetan Buddhism, a bodhisattva is a realized being who refuses to enter nirvana until all beings are enlightened. Legend has it that the goddess Tara was born from the tears of Avalokiteshvara, the bodhisattva of compassion. When Avalokiteshvara reached the top of the Red Hill in Lhasa, he could see the suffering of countless beings all across the vast landscape before him. Overcome with compassion, a teardrop welled up in his left eye, fell to the ground, and became the revered Tara.

In her iconography, Tara is often depicted as standing on a white lotus with one foot stepping into the world. The fact that she has one foot on the lotus and one in the world is meant to symbolize that she is the embodiment of compassion in action. I was drawn to Tara for this reason and because of a story I once read that relates a flat-out audacious vow she made to remain in the female form.

The story goes something like this. In one of her incarnations, Tara was a princess who earned great merit and respect among the monks of her local temple. They told her that they would pray for her to be reborn as a man, so she could spread the Buddha's teachings along with them. She responded by quoting the Buddha—"In all things, there is neither male nor female"—and vowed to remain in the female form for all her incarnations until all beings (including the monks) were freed of the illusion that a male body is necessary to reach enlightenment.[5] Even in her final lifetime when she attained Buddhahood, "then, too, I will be a woman," Tara said.[6]

Whatever work my soul continues to guide me to do, I know that at root I am here to model that the female body is not a limit, a hindrance, or a challenge when it comes to spiritual prowess. Ultimately, whatever form my soul-work takes, I will aim to maintain Tara's vow and her stance that the female body is holy. To me, Tara's message is that we are all at our most powerful when we move out into the world from within and we allow that place of connection and awareness to guide our every step. Even as we move further into the world, we remain perfectly rooted in one place—the heart.

DEEP GLADNESS

Christian minister Frederick Buechner writes, "The place God calls you to is the place where your deep gladness and the world's deep hunger meet."[7] For some of us, the path to find that intersection of our own happiness and the world's deep need is apparent. The trail has already been blazed, and the job or position or product line that can share our gifts and sustain our life already exists. It is there in plain sight. For others of us there is no template. It is something that we have to create ourselves.

I don't know what your soul-work in the world will look like, what form it will take, but I know it exists. I don't know what your soul will ask of you or what following your soul-voice will lead you to do. But I know that when you step into the world to be of service from a place of love, from the heart and not the ego, you align yourself with a force that's effortlessly miraculous. There is no greater abundance than the opportunity to experience that our capacity to give, when we give from the soul, is limitless.

This is the veil that lifts: our soul-work in the world is not ultimately about what it earns us in dollars or brand names or quantifiable things. Rather, it allows us to feel the invaluable sense of happiness and fulfillment that comes from knowing we have made our own unique contribution to the world. We receive the most when we give the love we are here to share. Soul-work is not something we have to go out and search for; it's getting the sacred chance to reveal exactly who we are.

Love.

The Seventh Veil

REVEAL Your Spiritual Community

*What would happen if one woman
told the truth about her life?
The world would split open.*

—MURIEL RUKEYSER

TOGETHER

We have all felt it at some point in our lives. It has
made us weep; it has made us laugh until our stomach
hurt or we peed a little; it has reminded us that we are
invincible. It has called back all the pieces of ourselves,
of our soul, that we somehow lost. It has allowed us to
feel that deliciously intimate bliss of being wildly alive,
as if we could skinny-dip in winter and fly through the
air on a swinging trapeze without worrying about a
net. We have all felt the power of what happens when
women come together.

Call it what you want—a gaggle of goddesses, a women's group, a femme flock, a power posse, a girl gang—it doesn't matter. All that matters is that you have women who will stand by you, women who will reflect back to you just how much you are and just how much you are here to share. There is no greater spiritual tool for revealing your soul than a bevy of women who believe in you.

We have been separated from ourselves for so long. Individually, we have endured such extreme distances from our own souls. And we have also had to withstand the collective pain of not trusting one another, of feeling we are pitted against one another. We are all different, but comparison is an unholy waste of our time. In the end, no difference stands a chance when we tell our truth to one another as women, with heart-stopping transparency and raw honesty.

If you tell me your story—that you long for love; that you're numb and lonely; that you lost your child; that you ache to have a child; that you've been abused; that you dream; that you cry at night wondering where the brave, little tom-girl is hiding; that you know there's another way to live; that you know there's more—my soul will root for you and want your freedom even more than my own.

No matter how briefly I know or encounter you, if you are getting spiritually naked and showing the real you, I will want every possible blessing to come your way. This is not unique to me; this is inherent in every woman I have ever known. The truth is, we want to love and support each other no matter our differences. The truth is, we know deep down that we're on the same sacred team and that our work right now is to love each other into wearing our wings.

Why is it so important to have spiritual community? You can never really forget who you are or what you came here to do if a dedicated group of women are with you on your pilgrimage, to unveil your own love to you. They will hold you to your truth with whatever love (or spiritual spanking) is necessary. They will love you when you have blocked your own love for yourself. They will feed you with their soul-talk and warm you with the fiery conversation of self-possessed women.

And they will feed you—literally. When you have deserted yourself, they will pick you up and put their home-cooked food in your mouth themselves if they have to. They will nurture you until you remember again that you want to be here, that life is good. They will help you laugh when you are least able to, and they will help you cry when you are trying to keep it locked inside you.

They will forgive you as quickly as you can ask for it. They will hold you steady as you do the treacherous work of going within, of meeting the audacity of the soul. They will be there as you take that love you have found within you and move it out into the world. They will hold your highest truth for you. They will pray with you. They will create rituals that comfort and support you. They will break dark chocolate with you.

They will look you in the eyes and wordlessly connect you to the power that has always existed, century after century, when we come together as women.

The Sisters of Sappho

The only criteria for entering our group were that you had to wear something silky, if only a scarf, and you had to come with a poem to read out loud. One night each month, we would darken the common room of our dorm and light several candles. We would have some music playing softly in the background (think Fiona Apple or the Cocteau Twins). We would uncork the red wine and then open the door to any woman interested in seeing what happens when we share the poetry that moves us most.

We called ourselves the Sisters of Sappho.

It all started in college when I came across the dictate that women in ancient Greece could not cut their hair, as a symbol and a reminder that females represent the Body. Men were to wear their hair short so that the forehead was exposed and out in the open, as the constant reminder that men represent the Mind. I responded by cutting my hair as short as I could get it while still covering my Neanderthal hairline and pointy ears and by starting the Sisters of Sappho.

We were studying Socrates, Plato, and Thales, and at some point in one of our class discussions, our professor mentioned Sappho. My back straightened and my eyes widened just to finally hear the name of a woman from antiquity. We weren't assigned to study her, but I did anyway. I learned that she was a Greek poet who lived independently on the island of Lesbos and basically had her own academy.

The 2nd-century philosopher Maximus of Tyre compared Sappho to Socrates: "They seem to me to have practiced love after their own fashion, she the love of women, and he of men."[1] And just as Socrates educated men, Sappho had some form of school or inner circle to educate or enlighten women. It was popular in the Victorian era to suggest that Sappho was the headmistress of a finishing school for girls in ancient Greece.

But scholars believe that Sappho's circle was far more similar to the Spartan *agelai,* age group, or to a *thiasos,* a sacred band.

A sacred band of sisters—this is what I wanted to create in honor of Sappho. Sappho's soul somehow freed her from the harsh, subordinate reality that society placed on females during her lifetime. Greek women in antiquity were just above the status of slaves, forbidden to own property, unable to choose their own husbands, lacking the right to vote and, in the event of divorce, not even able to keep their children. Despite all this oppression and limitation, Sappho found a way to exist outside of society's expectations of her gender and elevate the minds of other women as well.

There is very little known about Sappho that gives an accurate biography of her. The fragments of her poems on papyrus serve as the only remaining testament to her life. Her history, then, is a mosaic. When I realized this, when I stumbled across her life and its erasure, I felt as if my soul was tugging at my pant leg and begging to get my attention—to get me to see that this has been the case with women's history in every genre, especially when it comes to women and religion.

What the Sisters of Sappho gave me, aside from many unforgettable nights of love-drenched poetry, was the empowered conviction that if I longed for something, it was longing for me to find it. If I sensed a lack, a need, it's not that what I was longing for never existed, it's that its existence was not preserved, codified, honored, carried on. The Sisters of Sappho formed effortlessly. And every time we circled up, I remembered that this was nothing new—that women have been coming together in sacred bands since antiquity, since before recorded history.

After Sappho, I read *The Gnostic Gospels* by Elaine Pagels. *Gnostic* comes from the Greek word *gnosis,* meaning "knowledge." It is most often used to refer to the form of spiritual wisdom that arises from knowing our true self, from becoming enlightened.

I learned that there are gospels—over 50 of them—that are noncanonical texts representing the teachings of early Christians called Gnostics, who believed that salvation doesn't just come from worshipping Christ but also from direct knowing, from finding answers to spiritual questions within. The Gnostic path does not require the intermediation of the church to find salvation. Boom. There's no greater heresy than that.

The Gnostic Gospels were found at different times and in different places, but all of them were hidden away, since the inward journey threatened the efforts of the just-budding Christian Church to set itself up as the ultimate spiritual authority. Some of the church hierarchy obviously wanted all evidence of the Gnostic Gospels destroyed. But others felt the impulse to preserve them, to make sure that one day we could try to piece the fragments together to know for ourselves that the Bible was created by a process of selection, of editing; that there were many more gospels at the time to choose from; and that the stories and interpretations of Jesus's life and teachings didn't end with the Book of Revelation.

I read many of the texts and documents that comprise the Gnostic Gospels, including the Gospel of Thomas, the Gospel of Philip, the Gospel of Mary Magdalene, and the *Pistis Sophia,* which is a compilation of post-resurrection encounters between Jesus and Mary Magdalene. I read what I needed to know, not just what was assigned. The most valuable teaching I received in college was the knowledge that I was responsible for my own education.

At one of the last gatherings of the Sisters of Sappho before graduation, I read an excerpt from a poemlike text discovered among the Gnostic manuscripts at Nag Hammadi in 1945. It consists of a series of contradictions concerning the nature of the Divine Feminine. This form of poetry, made up of paradoxical statements, most likely draws from a tradition found in both Egyptian and Jewish communities, where a female deity—Isis and Sophia respectively—illustrates her virtues and advises those who seek her to strive to attain her. The text I read was originally composed in Greek but only survives in Coptic and is dated well before 350 C. E.; it was most likely written as early as the 2nd century. It is titled simply "Thunder Perfect Mind."

When I first came across the text in the library, I started crying before I even finished reading it. I didn't understand how, but I felt as if I had heard it before. Its contradictions, its cadences were familiar to me.

Initially, I felt angry that I had to dig for it—that this text wasn't presented to me as the voice of a female deity just as readily as the voice of the male deity had been engrained in me. But later I realized that this omission was essential to the education of who I am. I could never have missed it, not really. It would never have been lost to me. It's the voice of the Divine Feminine, and she lives mostly within me—far more so, anyway, than in manuscript fragments buried deep in Egyptian sands.

I was no doubt emboldened by the red wine, but for some reason I felt compelled to stand while reading this particular piece of poetry. I stood in the center of our circle on the low table that served as our altar. I took a deep breath and began to read each paradox as if it were tattooed on the underside of my skin. As I read each line, I claimed it as my own, as the sacred language that has always spoken to me. This is the truth that cannot be buried or forgotten. This is the Divine Feminine.

I am the first and the last.
I am the honored and the scorned,
I am the whore and the holy one.
I am the wife and the virgin.
I am the mother and the daughter.
I am a barren woman who has many children.
I have had many weddings,
And have taken no husband.
I am the silence that is incomprehensible
And insight whose memory is great.
I am the voice whose sounds are many.
I am the utterance of my own name.
Why have you hated me in your counsels?
I am the lamp of the heart.[2]

THE REDLADIES

Carol Lee Flinders in *At the Root of this Longing* tells us that the criteria for being "spiritual" have historically been based on the male experience. Theology has been created by and for the practice of men for millennia. The deprivations and denials required of a male monastic, or a monk, for example, have been a part of society's normal expectations for women: submission, solitude, starvation, sacrifice, and silence.

As a woman, then, what does it mean to be spiritual? This is what I wanted to find out. I wanted to know what being spiritual really meant to me as a woman and what spiritual practices I desired and needed in order to maintain a connection to the Divine.

Like the Sisters of Sappho, the REDLADIES banded together seamlessly. I had just returned to San Francisco from my second pilgrimage. I was meeting with my red ink daily, and I knew that the strange and mystical things that were happening to me had to be happening to other women as well. I knew I was a part of a movement, a zeitgeist. I knew that many other women were on their own version of a spiritual path to create for themselves what was missing in mainstream religion. I just had to find them.

There were only a handful of us REDLADIES that first year. We ate rice noodles and dark chocolate and nourished each other with the soul-talk we were all starving for. Sitting in a circle on my living room floor, we set intentions. We prayed together but in ways that we let ourselves uncover, not in ways we had been taught before. We gave ourselves the right to exercise our own wings, our own inner divinity.

We dared to get spiritually naked.

We created rituals for events or happenings that our religious traditions, for those of us who had any, didn't provide. Rituals that felt innate to us as women, rituals for calling in lovers and life partners, for work in the world that inspires us and fulfills us, and for preparing our bodies and busy lives for the arrival of a little one.

The REDLADIES let us live out the paradoxes that real lives contain without contradiction. We could be ardently spiritual, wanting to connect to the Divine within, and yet also be interested in feeling sexy. In other words, we didn't feel that wearing a nun's habit was necessary to prove that we were devoted to the Divine. We didn't need to wear a turtleneck to display our piousness; a deep V-neck with a peep of cleavage wouldn't disparage our nearness to the sacred.

We told the truth about our lives. We laughed. We sobbed our faces off. We exposed our deepest fears and our most debilitating wounds and saw them for what they really were—great huge manholes for the Divine to come barreling through. And we held with precious, ferocious love the highest possible vision for one another's lives.

The commonality between us that made us a sacred community was not that we shared the same religion. What made us soul-sisters was the simple fact that we were women in a world that didn't yet see our spiritual potential. Our connection was in our collective need to empower each other to experience what more traditional religion or secular culture had not provided. What bound us together was our need to experience ourselves and our lives as spiritual beings unapologetically in a body.

Wisdom Sophia is the female divinity of Gnosticism. She has a multitude of names: the Holy Spirit, the Universal Mother, She-of-the-left-hand-of-God (as opposed to Jesus who is of the right), the Womb, the Wife, the Virgin, the Revealer, the Psyche of the World, the Dove, the Moon, the Female Aspect of the Word. She is all of this without contradiction. In the *Pistis Sophia,* Jesus refers to her as "the All-Begetress."

This is what the REDLADIES gave me—the permission to inhabit all of me. There's no reason to define or delimit who I am or what I can become. I don't need to worry about trailblazing or breaking molds in order to carve out a life that is entirely my own. We have always had a model of the Divine Feminine that knew how to have it all.

THE DARK NIGHT

The spiritual phrase *the dark night of the soul* refers to a time when a person feels furthest from the Divine. It can last far longer than a night. Often, the night is a metaphor for a large portion of our lives when we feel disconnected from what's most holy to us. My dark night was both: it came in one night, and yet it revealed to me that I had lived much of my life in a kind of dark-ness—the kind of darkness that comes from believing I could ever be far from the soul.

My dark night looked something like this.

I was wide awake in the middle of the night, hold-ing a canister of Mace with a white-knuckled grip. Anxi-ety coursed through my veins. I was in my New York City apartment, sitting on my living room couch facing the front door, which was locked three times over. My one-year-old son was with his father, my Tall, Dark, and Handsome, who now lived separately from me. I was alone for the first time in years. I felt as if I were on the lookout, standing guard, waiting for something terrify-ing to happen or anticipating the return of something terrifying that had happened to me long ago.

The fear was so real that the locks and dead bolts provided no sense of comfort or protection. And the Mace—well, mostly I worried that if I had to use it I would end up unleashing it in the wrong direction. Ac-cording to my nervous system, I was prey. It didn't make any sense. It was without question the most irrational fear I had ever encountered. So here's what I did: I went into it. Rather than trying to avoid it, or drown it out by drinking red wine or watching *Sex and the City* reruns until all hours of the night or putting myself out with a sleeping pill, as I had on other nights since my T, D, and H had asked for a separation, I experienced the fear straight on.

I looked at the fear as if it was something objective—something outside of me. I stood above my life and looked at the ways fear had been directing and derailing me for longer than I had realized. I thought the fear had started after Flight U.S. Scare. But this was the same fear that as a teenager gave me a reputation in my family for "sleeping around." No one ever knew whose room I would seek out in the middle of the night. Sometimes just sleeping on the couch in the living room with the dog was more comforting than being in my own bedroom alone. Somehow I had blocked this out.

I was exhausted. And the exhaustion wasn't from being a single mom, as I sometimes complained. It wasn't from lack of sleep or the stress of being on my own. This exhaustion went much deeper. It went into my bloodstream and deep into my bones. I was exhausted from letting this fear live in me for so long.

I was at an end. So I picked up my red pen, and I asked quickly, desperately:

What do I fear the most?

The answer I wrote:

> *your only fear is to be separated from me.*
> *fear puts veils between us.*
> *i am here. i have never left.*
> *i am your freedom.*
> *i am your beloved.*

My ultimate fear was not being abused again, although I recognized that I was experiencing the same fear I had experienced that night as a little girl. It had lived in me all these years. What I feared most, however, was the dissociation of my body and soul.

I had exhausted myself with the effort of trying to protect myself. I was tired from the weight of the belief I had carried with me most of my life that I could prevent something horrible from happening to me. I was trying to prevent pain and suffering. I was operating under the false belief that I was in control and that I was the only one carrying myself through the storms. And rather than make me feel safe or less afraid, believing that I could control my life and protect myself terrified me. I felt powerless and drained.

I wasn't alone. I had never been alone. And I had never been in control. Even in my darkest moments—especially then—fierce love from my soul had and would always rise up to meet me. And although I was physically by myself, I was flanked by an unseen crowd. I was surrounded by the spirit of all of those who love me. We all are. At all times.

This is the revelation that changed me. I didn't fear anything external to me. I feared separation from the one source of love I can actually never be without—my soul. No matter what comes my way, this is a power that no single event no matter how devastating can ever take from me.

And how did I realize this? How did I finally get to the root of my fear?

The first week after moving into my own apartment with my son, my GAD returned in full force. It had been so long since I'd had a panic attack, but wow, are they convincing! I called my spiritual mentor right away.

"The fear comes so intensely some nights, and it feels so frickin' real," I told her through tears, "that I'm starting to dread going to sleep at all."

"Girl," she said in her long, drawn-out way, "you know what you need to do."

I did. But I stayed silent and played dumb, in order to have more time to come up with excuses.

"You have to face this!" she continued with excitement, as if this were the greatest possible thing that could have come my way. "You have to go within and create the space for this fear to reveal itself once and for all."

I replied with what I imagined to be my greatest excuse: "I'm a single mom now. I can't just have a sudden urban retreat in my apartment and meditate for three days! I can't just tell my baby's dad to come get him!"

The line went pin-drop silent.

Crap, I thought to myself. *She knows that's not true. I could do it. My T, D, and H would understand. He would take our son for a few days in a heartbeat.* This was when my greatest excuse became my greatest reason for making sure I faced this fear, that I finally got to the root of it: my son and the ferocious love I have for him.

I lived sandwiched between two REDLADIES. One, a Serbian woman who became a theologian because she couldn't become a priest in her Eastern Orthodox tradition, brought me meals in Tupperware during those several days I went into deep meditation. The other, a fiery, redheaded Texan, would send me texts at just the right moments to remind me of who I am to her, which is the highest version of me. I had to face my deepest fear on my own, from within, but the women in my life made sure I didn't forget that no one wins her freedom alone. As a pilgrim, I had made my vows; in a sense I had married my own soul. But the women in my life are the reason I can keep those vows. Remain faithful. They hold me to them.

A SACRED SPACE

The secret ingredient that goes into a potent, powerful REDLADIES gathering is an invisible presence, a magic that comes only if I hold the space for it to join us. I can't contrive or control it. It comes effortlessly and with ease when the sincerity of love fills the room.

As the facilitator, all I have to do is let love be real enough, present enough that I can feel it sitting next to me as palpably as I can feel the women who have gathered around me. I imagine filling the room with it. Or I picture it as a giant golden egg that surrounds the group, its shell protective enough to let in only positive thoughts and porous enough to release any fear or negativity. I let love know that not only is it welcome, it reigns.

I have always lit a red candle as a symbolic way to open the door for love. And I say a prayer right before a REDLADIES gathering or group phone call starts. I ask for my soul-voice to guide my every word and for Divine Love to allow the highest possible outcome to unfold for us all.

A minyan in Judaism is a group of no less than ten men needed in order to perform certain rituals and ceremonies, especially public prayer. To start a women's spiritual group, all you need are two women.

A space is made sacred because of what you share; you don't need to meet in a church, synagogue, or temple. We create holy space by the quality of our presence, by who we dare to be with each other, not by our external surroundings. An Applebee's, perfect. A cool nightclub where you'll be left alone in a corner over some red wine or sparkling pomegranate juice, great. A living room, a diner, a basement with gym equipment, all good. Only two women are needed, and if you allow it, only love will be present. Then just expect magic.

According to the REDLADIES themselves, this is what REDLADIES is all about: "holding space without judgment as we each find our own voice to tell our own story"; "coming home to my body"; "access to a force of love far greater than I ever experienced"; "hearing and listening to a sacred part of myself, a voice that I regularly heard and listened to at a much younger age"; "permission to yearn"; "feminine power"; "acceptance and pure light"; "foregoing fear and finding the faith to seek my highest calling"; "digging deeper and seeking the Divine in my soul without apology"; "creating a safe space to share openly and remember the Divine."

Telling the Truth

Risks are far more fun to take when you have a group of women who serve as your soul's safety net to catch you should that risk send you into a free fall. That I have lady loves in my life—women who inspire and spur me on—has been my one constant. It has allowed me the rare opportunity of transforming any trauma in my life into an adventure.

I thrive through the unexpected, the curveballs, the out of the blues because I have women who know how to wink at my soul and ask me to take this next turn as the angel I am, no matter how human I need to be as well. I credit the presence of the REDLADIES in my life with giving me the sacred space to win back my body and to hear and follow the voice of my soul. I know I would never have found my own love within me without their love surrounding me.

Abigail Disney's documentary *Pray the Devil Back to Hell* undid me. In the face of the raw, honest presence of love in the film, every defense or emotional wall in me dissolved. The film documents the revolutionary power of women coming together in spiritual community. As I saw how their love and compassion for each other transformed into spiritual activism, I was reminded that there is no such thing as being separate. It's the illusion that we're separate that keeps us from realizing our potential.

The Muslim and Christian women of Liberia, once divided by their faiths, came together to share their stories of what they had endured during civil war in their country. They shared their grief and their trauma as women who had been raped, whose husbands and children had been maimed and murdered. The imperative to join together to demand peace trumped their religious differences. They realized they could use those differences to gain more leverage in their work for peace.

Coming together as mothers, sisters, grandmothers, wives, aunts, and daughters, they found that their collective power as women was utterly unstoppable. These courageous women, Muslim and Christian, began to meet every day in front of the Presidential Palace in Monrovia, wearing all white. Crying and mourning, singing and laughing, they stood resolutely as a unified voice of peace and freedom for all of Liberia.

I was fortunate enough to meet Abigail Disney and ask her what personally compelled her to produce this documentary. Her response was riveting. She said that when she looked for footage of the Liberian women's peace movement, it was like sifting through a pile of hay for the proverbial needle. She had to search through endless images of war—of disfigured bodies and the unholy landscape of carnage created by powerful warlords pitted against each other—to find anything documenting the women's efforts.

Abigail Disney made this film to prevent the erasure of women's history and women's power that has gone on for centuries. She wanted to make sure we never forget what took place—that women came together as women, told the truth about their lives, and prayed for each other and for peace, that they took nonviolent action together and brought a horrific war to its knees.

One of the most significant reasons for the presence of the Divine Feminine now is to heal women's relationships—not only with themselves but also with each other. As the poet Adrienne Rich once put it, "The connections between and among women are the most feared, the most problematic, and the most potentially transforming force on the planet."[3]

THE SOUL EMBODIED

The pilgrimages I went on revealed to me that true love exists within. But the women in my life—their love, their honesty—are the reason I have been able to integrate that truth to the point of living it daily. They reminded me, even when it was so hard to hear, that my soul is what I longed for when this journey began. This was the love I longed to meet and stay connected to no matter what came my way. The only thing I ardently and truly feared was losing this connection I now have with my soul. This is why I have suffered—to know this direct connection to what is eternal in me, to know that my own true source of love is found within.

Our actions inspire and affect those around us. Toni Morrison has said that, "The function of freedom is to free someone else."[4] We are here with and for each other. Our ultimate task, according to Martin Luther King, Jr., is to create "the beloved community." This is a community bound together by the Golden Rule—to love another is to love ourselves.

When we come together as a spiritual community— as a long-lost, brazen band of soul-sisters, priestesses, miracle workers, healers, freelance mystics, financial divas, and "femme-preneurs"—we can remember with as little effort as an exhale that it is a sacred imperative to honor that powerful little girl within, to cherish her vulnerability as a strength, to experience her vast capacity to love, and to take action with her unfaltering faith that absolutely anything is possible.

In the company of women, it's easier for each of us to remember our own truth. We remember that our lives depend on our capacity to drop all facades and pretenses. We remember the bliss of just accepting that we are here to be ourselves. And we remember, together, that the most powerful place for us to be, even if it is sometimes terrifying, is fully in our body, so that we can move with the vulnerability and compassion of a broken-open heart.

On a recent flight, I danced all the way back to my seat after using the bathroom. This dancing where I had been most afraid is the evidence of a freedom I knew as a little girl. I know it now again, for the first time.

The final veil lifts as the desire for all of us to remember the language of the heart, a language of the soul embodied. Then, in the words of French philosopher Hélène Cixous, we can recall together the words of the "language that women speak when no one is there to correct them."[5] We can release the weight of thinking we are on our own. Your soul is with you, is you . . . you are not separate from it. And we are not separate from each other. We are all connected. We are never alone.

Benediction

The ultimate authority of my life is not the Bible; it is not confined between the covers of a book . . . It is not from a source outside of myself. My ultimate authority is the divine voice in my own soul. Period. It is not something written by men and frozen in time.

— SUE MONK KIDD

Here is what I want most for you.

I want you to own every one of your stories—all the happy and sordid things that have happened to you so far. Know that you are the one holding the pen that creates or delimits what now unfolds for you. I want you to be able to begin again, right now, if that's what you choose. You can clear the slate, wipe everything off the table, and open the blinds to the white crispness of what's next for you. You do not have to be who you have been. You get to choose this adventure story; it's yours. You are the author. Be the lead, the main character, the one with a happy ending that hasn't been done before, the one that's entirely your own.

I want you to love your body enough to be able to be present in it. I want you to know how good it feels to refuse to abandon or betray it. I want you to look at your face, your thighs, or your hands without criticism or any thoughts of comparison. I want you to look at your body with love, with gratitude, even if you have to fake it at first. I don't want you to spend another second wasting your precious energy on what your body is not. I want you to accept that it is a blessing, no matter how ill or broken. Your body is your chance to be here. I want you to love it because it's yours. I want you to refuse anyone who will not treat your body with the reverence it deserves. I want you—for all of us—to honor your body as if it is a holy temple entrusted only to you.

I want you to be able to take the voice of your soul, the voice of love within you, as the ultimate authority in your life, especially when someone else is imposing their version of what's highest or best for you. I want you to be able to remain calm, look them square in the face, and simply say, "Thank you for your advice or your [fill in the blank], but I can hear loud and clear what is true for me." And I don't want you to ever apologize for knowing what's true for you and taking action on it.

I want you to be able to give your own love to yourself at will, spontaneously, at necessary moments in your everyday life. I want you to be able to connect to the love your soul contains wherever you are—folding laundry, traveling to work, or changing a diaper. This way you'll know that you don't have to be anyone other than who you are to receive love and that there's nowhere you need to go. (Nowhere, that is, except within.)

I want you to be able to be truly brave—to have the courage to forgive yourself and others in your life so that no excuses remain to keep you from receiving your own love. I want you to know that what you do, you do out of love for yourself, not in order to be loved. I want you to know that being loved is not earned, it's innate. We only need to love ourselves more to bring more love into our lives.

I want you to feel that you are powerful beyond conscious reasoning. You are a mystical being, a soul choosing to inhabit a body. I don't want you to hide any aspect of your being, not just for your life but for mine also. If you allow your strangeness to strut around in broad daylight, you invite mine to come out to play, too. We are only as limited as our own imagination. Tether your imagination to the love inside you, and there's nothing you can't imagine for your life. Healing and miracles come from this place that allows us to make believe. I want you to feel the magic that's rubbing elbows with you in this moment. I want your life to hum with the signs and curious synchronicities that give you those jolts, zaps, and zings that let you feel wildly alive and intricately woven into the mysterious tapestry of what's Divine. I want your direct connection to the Divine to be your soul's medicine cabinet, where you heal and renew.

I want you to protect and covet the gifts of love you have to share and to trust your soul enough to let it lead you. I want you to feel the utterly priceless sensation of giving away the love you possess through whatever work your soul desires for you to do. I want you to experience just how limitless Divine Love is—that it comes from an inner well that no one has access to but you. I want you to be free to do what it is you have come here to do. I want you to be able to take yourself lightly even as you take your contribution in the world seriously. I want you to hold on tight to your vision in the face of ridicule and doubt, whether from inside or outside of you. I want you to dare to do what is coiled up at the base of your spine. Those ardent desires and dreams are there for a reason, as if you were born with them already inside you. I want you to experience the truth that you matter, your voice matters—that your one life can tip the world's scale in love's favor. But only if you dare to use it.

I want you to be surrounded by women who see you. Women who help you live out your highest potential by reflecting that potential back to you when you lose sight of it. I want them to help you have compassion toward what you might first judge as mistakes and find where you are most unique and love the hell out of your strangeness. And I want them to let you live with the thrill, not the threat, of the unknown, morphing what you feared to do before into a dare, a challenge, an adventure. I want them to help you see that you can risk it all, because there is only one true asset you have in this life, and it's something you can never lose: the Divine Love inside you. So don't wait another second: give it all away.

I want you to be able to say with ease and conviction that you know who you are, that you know that aspect of you that never changes, even as everything changes around you. I want you to know that we are not separate, you and I. I want you to know that you will never happen again. I want your life to become astoundingly simple, stripped down to the only task the soul asks of you: be the love that you are.

I now have what I became a pilgrim to find. I have a way—no matter where I am, no matter what my state of mind—to connect to that fleur-de-lis at the center of the labyrinth, that flower of fire and light in the core of my heart, to connect to the limitless love the soul contains.

I have same-olds in spades. I have a feisty community of women who spur me on to keep revealing all of me. I trust life enough not to control it, and I have long since given over any plans for what's next to that quiet, unassuming soul-voice inside me. It, being Divine, knows the way. All I need to do is sit back and enjoy the ride. What I need will always trump what I think I want. What comes my way if I am present and grateful for what I already have in this moment will always blow the roof off what I could imagine.

Showing up, being fiercely present, raw, naked, and real with who I am, is all I need to do. I can experience fear and all of its compelling physical sensations but choose love instead. I can choose, again and again, to be present in my body and to claim it as home. Because then, and only then, can I hand my soul a megaphone and hear the eternal truths that are tirelessly whispered from within this sacred body.

life will always ask you to choose.
will it be fear or love?
one at a time, they live inside you.
fear and love cannot coexist.
you are here again. it is time to choose.
will it be fear or love?
let love move fully into you.
let it crowd out what has lived in you, uninvited.
let love be you.
you were never meant to be afraid.
you were only meant to wake up—to be aware.
every prophet and priestess has known this.

true love is within.
fear is only fear. but love is everything.
only love is real.
this is union—to merge with the love inside you.
to meet with the one love that has never left you.
take my hand.
you have never been alone.
your only fear is to be separated from me.
fear puts veils between us.
i am here. i have never left.
i am your freedom.
i am your beloved.
the locks fall from every door,
every cage that has contained you opens.
be who you are, the world needs you.
you remember me.
i am you.
you are free.

Endnotes

Introduction

1. Marguerite Porete, *The Mirror of Simple Souls* (Mahwah, New Jersey: Paulist Press, 1993), 162.

The First Veil

1. Jalal al-Din Rumi, *The Essential Rumi,* trans. Coleman Barks with John Moyne (San Francisco, HarperSanFrancisco, 1995), 131.

The Second Veil

1. Marion Woodman, *The Pregnant Virgin: A Process of Psychological Transformation* (Toronto, ON: Inner City Books, 1985), 122.
2. Ibid.
3. Ibid., 100.
4. Ibid., 121.
5. Ibid., 122.
6. Saint Teresa of Avila, *Interior Castle,* trans. and ed. E. Allison Peers (New York: Image Books/Doubleday, 1989), 31.
7. Karen L. King, *The Gospel of Mary of Magdala: Jesus and the First Woman Apostle* (Santa Rosa, CA: Polebridge Press, 2003), 15.
8. Ibid., 54.
9. Ibid., 55–6.
10. Ntozake Shange, "Lady in Red," from *For Colored Girls Who Have Considered Suicide When the Rainbow is Enuf* (New York: Scribner, 1997), 63.

11. Marion Woodman, *The Pregnant Virgin*, 85.

The Third Veil

1. Elizabeth Gilbert, *Eat, Pray, Love: One Woman's Search for Everything Across Italy, India, and Indonesia* (New York: Viking, 2006), 16.
2. Ibid.

The Fourth Veil

1. "Silence, Sirens, Bells, and Lennon," in *The Guardian*, September 15, 2011, http://www.guardian.co.uk/world/2001/sep/15/september11.usa16?INTCMP=SRCH

2. Ian McEwan, "Only Love and then Oblivion," in *The Guardian*, September 15, 2011, http://www.guardian.co.uk/world/2001/sep/15/september11.politicsphilosophyandsociety2?INTCMP=SRCH

3. Rainer Maria Rilke, *Rilke on Love and Other Difficulties*, trans. John J. L. Mood (New York: W. W. Norton, 1975), 30–1.

4. Ibid., 35.

5. Rainer Maria Rilke, *Duino Elegies & the Sonnets to Orpheus*, trans. Stephen Mitchell (New York: Vintage International, 2009), 141.

6. "The *Physiologus*, a bestiary written in the 3rd century A.D. in Alexandria, compiled myths of various species. It included the ferocious unicorn, which could not be captured by hunters but which could be lured to the side of a virgin and captured as it slept with its head in her lap." Margaret Starbird, *The Woman with the Alabaster Jar: Mary Magdalene and the Holy Grail*, (Rochester, VT: Bear and Company, 1993), 133.

7. Marion Woodman, *The Pregnant Virgin*, 133.

8. Margaret Starbird, *The Woman with the Alabaster Jar*, 135.

9. Ibid., 137.

10. Ibid., 143.

11. Ibid., 159

12. David Noel Freedman, ed., *The Anchor Bible Dictionary*, vol. 6 (New York: Doubleday, 1992), 154.

13. Ibid.

14. Ibid., Sermon 83:4.

15. Marion Woodman, *The Pregnant Virgin*, 85.

16. Ibid., 109.

17. Simone Weil, *Waiting for God*, trans. Emma Craufurd (New York: G. P. Putnam, 1951), 24.

18. Ibid.

19. George Herbert, "Love," in introduction to Simone Weil, *Waiting for God,* 25.

20. Leslie Fiedler, introduction to Simone Weil, *Waiting for God,* 34.

21. Ibid., 18.

22. Ibid.

23. Hal Taussig, "Detours at the Intersection of Church and Sex," *USQR* [Union Theological Seminary Review], vol. 57, 111.

24. Luce Irigaray, *The Speculum of the Other Woman* (Ithaca, NY: Cornell University Press, 1985), 133.

25. Lynda McClanahan, in David M. Carr, *The Erotic Word: Sexuality, Spirituality, and the Bible* (New York: Oxford University Press, 2003), 147.

26. Marie-Louise von Franz, *On Dreams and Death: A Jungian Interpretation* (La Salle, IL: Open Court, 1998), 44.

27. Marie-Louise von Franz, *Alchemy: An Introduction to the Symbolism and the Psychology* (Toronto, ON: Inner City Books, 1980), 179.

28. Marie-Louise von Franz, *On Dreams and Death,* 44.

29. Marie-Louise von Franz, *Alchemy,* 189.

30. Ibid. 189.

31. Simone Weil, *Waiting for God,* trans. Emma Craufurd (New York: G. P. Putnam, 1951), 15.

32. Jean-Yves Leloup, *The Gospel of Mary Magdalene* (Rochester, VT: Inner Traditions, 2002), 74.

33. Ibid., 72.

34. Ibid., 102.

35. Ibid., xxii.

36. Jane Schaberg, *The Resurrection of Mary Magdalene* (New York: Continuum, 2002), 185.

The Fifth Veil

1. Jeffrey Kripal, *Roads of Excess, Palaces of Wisdom* (Chicago: University of Chicago Press, 2001), 311.

2. Saint Teresa of Avila, *Interior Castle,* 213–14.

3. Marie-Louise von Franz, *Alchemy,* 126.

4. Ibid., 127.

5. Ibid., 168.

6. Ibid.

7. Ibid., 172.

8. Ibid., 173.

9. Ibid., 174.

10. Saint Augustine, *Confessions*, trans. Henry Chadwick (New York: Oxford University Press, 1991), 201.

11. Ibid.

12. Ibid., 278.

13. Ibid.

14. Rainer Maria Rilke, *Rilke on Love and Other Difficulties*, 99.

15. Ibid., 98.

16. Ibid.

The Sixth Veil

1. Gospel of Saint Thomas 70:1–2.

2. Song of Songs 5:2.

3. Gospel of Saint Thomas 70:1–2.

4. Anne Lamott, *Bird by Bird: Some Instructions on Writing and Life* (New York and San Francisco: Pantheon, 1994), 236.

5. Lama Tsultrim Allione, *Women, Buddhism and the Absolute and Relative Truth*, http://taramandala.org/article/women-buddhism-and -the-absolute-and-relative-truth/

6. His Holiness the Dalai Lama, address at the Harmonia Mundi Contemplative Congress, Newport Beach, CA, October 1989.

7. Frederick Buechner, *Wishful Thinking* (New York: HarperCollins, 1993), 119.

The Seventh Veil

1. Maximus of Tyre, quoted in *Same-Sex Desire in the English Renaissance. A Sourcebook of Texts, 1470–1650* (New York and London: Routledge, 2004), 246.

2. "Thunder Perfect Mind," in *The Nag Hammadi Scriptures: The International Edition* (New York: HarperCollins, 2007), 372–77.

3. Adrienne Rich, "Disloyal to Civilization," in *On Lies, Secrets, and Silence* (New York and London: W. W. Norton, 1979), 279.

4. Martha Beck, *Set It Free*, September 15, 2011, http://marthabeck. com/2011/09/set-it-free/

5. Hélène Cixous, "Coming to Writing," in *"Coming to Writing" and Other Essays*, ed. and trans. Deborah Jenson (Cambridge, MA and London: Harvard University Press, 1992), 21.

Acknowledgments

I have been writing and rewriting this section of the book in my heart for years. And I see now that it wasn't just a silly little thing I did while washing my hair or riding the subway. Having gratitude and love for everyone along my path is the path.

Writing this book has been a soul-assignment I've carried with me for most of my life. Believing in my soul-voice enough to actually share it has taken so much love and wisdom from so many. What follows is my attempt at thanking as many as I can without writing a book of equal length to name every force of love that made this book possible.

I want to start by thanking you—my reader. Your desire to read this book was the calling I answered by writing it.

I also want to acknowledge my deep gratitude for all of the women who create and contribute to feminist theology and the women's spirituality movement. My path has had so many signposts because of the hard-won wisdom you laid out before me. Thank you.

To all of the REDLADIES from the past to the present, thank you for reflecting back to me the Divine Love

I am here to be, and for fiercely holding with me the highest intentions I have for my life. May we always break dark chocolate together and free our souls.

To my shaman, Wendi Raw, and to my spiritual mentor, Rha Goddess, thank you for holding a space so vast and concrete that I could see all of me, from the dark to light.

To my mom, Margaret Seelbach Wheeler, thank you for the passion and temerity you gave me, for the way you modeled to me that the holiest thing we can do is speak our truth, and for always singing the refrain, "I believe in angels . . . " from ABBA's "I Have a Dream." I'm so grateful that I don't need to believe anymore, I know. Smile.

To Elizabeth "Lulu" Wheeler, Michael Seelbach, Dan Kosh, and David Stone, thank you for our monthly family dinners in NYC, and for being there for me on otherwise lonely nights and holidays without my son. And to all of my family members, especially Kristyn Gorton, Andrew Watterson, David Watterson, John Wheeler, Tracy Wheeler, Cathy Watterson, Heather Gibbs Flett, and Chad Gibbs, thank you all for your love and support and for reminding me of how unimaginably rich we are because we have each other.

To Joseph Nicholas Masi, thank you for being the most amazing co-parent an indie mom could ever hope to have, for believing in my writing from the first story I ever shared, for helping me learn to fly, and for being such a magnificent father to our son.

To Shai Watterson Masi, thank you for being the greatest gift in my life, for making me laugh when I need to most, for mushing your little face into mine as your own signature kiss, for having imaginary dogs that make our apartment feel more like home, and for reminding me again and again that we are here to love and be loved, nothing more.

To all my ladyloves of REVEAL, especially Dawn Copeland and Joanna Lindenbaum, my midwives for the conference, Gabrielle Bernstein, Vanessa Cordoniu, Ophira and Tali Edut, Rha Goddess, Sheherazade Jafari, Valarie Kaur, Linda Kay Klein, Courtney E. Martin, Kate Northrup, Manisha Thakor, Latham Thomas, Alisa Vitti, and Jamia Wilson, thank you for your unfaltering, empowering love, support and spiritual cheerleading.

To my literary agent Tracy Brown, thank you for believing in my initial idea for *Reveal* to share the stories of the next generation of women's spirituality, for always having our literary meetings at French cafes, and for being a sincere voice of support for my writing.

To my editor at Hay House Patty Gift, thank you for attending the REVEAL at Urban Zen in 2011, for responding to my timely proposal for the book with passion, for gently, yet expertly, encouraging me to just reveal my own story in *Reveal,* and for becoming a trusted guide through this publishing process, and one of my most treasured friends.

To Sally Mason, Laura Gray, Erin Dupree, Quressa Robinson, Mollie Langer, Michelle Pilley, and everyone at Hay House who played a part in making *Reveal* as polished and powerful as I have always hoped, thank you.

To the entire Hay House family, especially Louise Hay and Reid Tracy, thank you for providing a spiritual misfit and pilgrim like me a place to thrive, for giving my soul-voice the widest possible wingspan, and for creating a community of deeply loving souls.

To my publicist Jane Wesman, thank you for wanting to take *Reveal* on with enthusiasm. And thank you for this gem—"You'll meet who you love while doing what you love."

To Donna Freitas, thank you for being the most beloved friend, for meeting with me chapter by chapter over the best possible red wine and in the sexiest restaurants NYC has to offer, and for loving me with a loyalty and a devotion that is as fierce as my own.

To Paul William Morris, thank you for being my most devoted reader for more than a decade from *The Blue Jean Buddha* to epic e-mails, postcards, and book jacket covers scrawled in my nearly illegible red ink, for being there when I needed you most, for our magic, our bridge building, and most of all for being my Ged. If not for the invisible yet trustworthy hand you offered me, I might never have made it from out of the Labyrinth.

To Brooke Elise Axtell, thank you for your passionate support of *Reveal,* for being a Women's Media Center sister, and for your vital feedback on the 2nd and 4th veils.

And to every person, pilgrimage site, and source of Divine Love that is a part of this book: Sue Monk Kidd, the shaman, Carl Jung, Marguerite Porete, Mary Magdalene, China Galland, the Black Madonna of Montserrat, the goddess Kali, La, the goddess Isis, my T, D, & H, my first (and last) Unitarian Sunday school teacher, all of the courageous teens of St. E's, St. Teresa of Avila, Marion Woodman, the Black Madonna of Vassiviere, Saint Sarah-La-Kali, the woman with the mapped face, Karen King, Jesus Christ, Ntozake Shange, Emily Dickinson, the Lone Ranger, a little girl with huge light named India, Anand, Anandamayi Ma, Simone Weil, Rilke, R. Kelly, Elizabeth Gilbert, Marianne Williamson, Will, John Lennon, Ian

McEwan, the Black Madonna of Le Puy, Jean-Pierre, Jean Yves Leloup, Gita Mallasz, Jane Schaberg, Jeanette Winterson, Jeffrey Kripal, Taitetsu Unno, Martha Beck, Karen Vogel and Vicki Noble's MotherPeace Tarot Deck, Amma, Satya, the little girl with fire red socks and a hole in the heel, the baby girl with LOVE written across her t-shirt, the Black Madonna of Einsiedeln, Martha Graham, St. Augustine, Paracelsus, Marie-Louise Von Franz, Caroline Myss, the NICU staff of New York Presbyterian Hospital, Lupe, Annabelle, Rivka, Elaine Pagels, Hyun Kyung Chung, Lucky, Liam Neeson, Anne Lamott, the goddess Tara, Muriel Rukeyser, Sappho, the sisters of Sappho, Carol Lee Flinders, Adrienne Rich, Toni Morrison, Martin Luther King, Jr., thank you for being spiritual teachers on my path to cultivate and expand my capacity to love—or said again—thank you for inspiring me to reveal in my own life Marguerite Porete's truth that, "Love has no beginning, no end, and no limit, and I am nothing except Love."

ABOUT THE AUTHOR

Meggan Watterson is a spiritual mentor, speaker and scholar of the Divine Feminine who inspires women to live from the audacity and authenticity of the voice of their soul.

She is the facilitator of the REDLADIES, a spiritual community that encourages women to reclaim their bodies as sacred and to be led by the soul-voice inside them without compromise or apology. (Some break bread together; REDLADIES break dark chocolate.) Meggan is the founder of REVEAL, a women's spirituality event that is a triumvirate of one part fiery soul-voices, one part ritual and one part dance party. She received a Master of Theological Studies from Harvard Divinity School and a Master of Divinity from Union Theological Seminary at Columbia University. She lives in New York City with her son. Find her on Facebook (Meggan Jane Watterson) and join the *Reveal* community by going to the REVEAL Facebook page.

www.megganwatterson.com
@megganwatterson